THE MOST EFFECTIVE ANTI-INFLAMMATORY RECIPES 2022

MOUTH-WATERING RECIPES TO BOOST YOUR HEALTH

SANDRA THOMAS

Table of Contents

Meatball Taco Bowls Ingredients: 15

Directions: 16

Avocado Pesto Zoodles With Salmon Servings: 4 18

Ingredients: 18

Directions: 18

Turmeric-spiced Sweet Potatoes, Apple, And Onion With Chicken 20

Ingredients: 20

Seared Herbed Salmon Steak Servings: 4 22

Ingredients: 22

Directions: 22

Tofu And Italian-seasoned Summer Vegetables Servings: 4 24

Ingredients: 24

Directions: 24

Strawberry And Goat Cheese Salad Ingredients: 26

Directions: 26

Turmeric Cauliflower And Cod Stew Servings: 4 28

Ingredients: 28

Directions: 28

Walnuts And Asparagus Delight Servings: 4 30

Ingredients: 30

Directions: 30

Alfredo Zucchini Pasta Ingredients: 31

Directions: 31

Quinoa Turkey Chicken Ingredients: 33

- Directions: 34
- Garlic & Squash Noodles Servings: 4 36
- Ingredients: 36
- Directions: 37
- Steamed Trout With Red Bean And Chili Salsa Servings: 1 38
- Ingredients: 38
- Directions: 39
- Sweet Potato And Turkey Soup Servings: 4 40
- Ingredients: 40
- Directions: 41
- Miso Broiled Salmon Servings: 2 42
- Ingredients: 42
- Directions: 42
- Simply Sautéed Flaky Fillet Servings: 6 44
- Ingredients: 44
- Directions: 44
- Pork Carnitas Servings: 10 45
- Ingredients: 45
- Directions: 46
- White Fish Chowder With Vegetables 47
- Servings: 6 To 8 47
- Ingredients: 47
- Directions: 47
- Lemony Mussels Servings: 4 49
- Ingredients: 49
- Directions: 49
- Lime & Chili Salmon Servings: 2 50

Ingredients: 50

Directions: 50

Cheesy Tuna Pasta Servings: 3-4 51

Ingredients: 51

Directions: 51

Coconut Crusted Fish Strips Servings: 4 53

Ingredients: 53

Directions: 54

Mexican Fish Servings: 2 55

Ingredients: 55

Directions: 55

Trout With Cucumber Salsa Servings: 4 57

Ingredients: 57

Lemon Zoodles With Shrimp Servings: 4 59

Ingredients: 59

Directions: 59

Crispy Shrimp Servings: 4 61

Ingredients: 61

Directions: 61

Broiled Sea Bass Servings: 2 62

Ingredients: 62

Directions: 62

Salmon Cakes Servings: 4 63

Ingredients: 63

Directions: 63

Spicy Cod Servings: 4 64

Ingredients: 64

Directions: 64

Smoked Trout Spread Servings: 2 65

Ingredients: 65

Directions: 65

Tuna And Shallots Servings: 4 67

Ingredients: 67

Directions: 67

Lemon Pepper Shrimp Servings: 2 68

Ingredients: 68

Directions: 68

Hot Tuna Steak Servings: 6 69

Ingredients: 69

Directions: 69

Cajun Salmon Servings: 2 71

Ingredients: 71

Directions: 71

Quinoa Salmon Bowl With Vegetables 72

Servings: 4 72

Ingredients: 72

Crumbed Fish Servings: 4 74

Ingredients: 74

Directions: 74

Simple Salmon Patties Servings: 4 75

Ingredients: 75

Directions: 76

Popcorn Shrimp Servings: 4 77

Ingredients: 77

Directions: 78

Spicy Baked Fish Servings: 5 79

Ingredients: 79

Directions: 79

Paprika Tuna Servings: 4 80

Ingredients: 80

Directions: 80

Fish Patties Servings: 2 81

Ingredients: 81

Directions: 81

Seared Scallops With Honey Servings: 4 82

Ingredients: 82

Directions: 82

Cod Fillets With Shiitake Mushrooms Servings: 4 84

Ingredients: 84

Directions: 84

Broiled White Sea Bass Servings: 2 86

Ingredients: 86

Directions: 86

Baked Tomato Hake Servings: 4-5 87

Ingredients: 87

Directions: 87

Seared Haddock With Beets Servings: 4 89

Ingredients: 89

Heartfelt Tuna Melt Servings: 4 91

Ingredients: 91

Directions: 91

Lemon Salmon With Kaffir Lime Servings: 8 93

    Ingredients: 93

    Directions: 93

Tender Salmon In Mustard Sauce Servings: 2 95

    Ingredients: 95

    Directions: 95

Crab Salad Servings: 4 97

    Ingredients: 97

    Directions: 97

Baked Salmon With Miso Sauce Servings: 4 98

    Ingredients: 98

    Directions: 98

Herb-coated Baked Cod With Honey Servings: 2 100

    Ingredients: 100

    Directions: 100

Parmesan Cod Mix Servings: 4 102

    Ingredients: 102

    Directions: 102

Crispy Garlic Shrimp Servings: 4 103

    Ingredients: 103

    Directions: 103

Creamy Sea Bass Mix Servings: 4 104

    Ingredients: 104

    Directions: 104

Cucumber Ahi Poke Servings: 4 105

    Ingredients: 105

Minty Cod Mix Servings: 4 107

Ingredients: 107

Directions: 107

Lemony & Creamy Tilapia Servings: 4 109

Ingredients: 109

Directions: 109

Fish Tacos Servings: 4 111

Ingredients: 111

Directions: 112

Ginger Sea Bass Mix Servings: 4 113

Ingredients: 113

Directions: 113

Coconut Shrimp Servings: 4 114

Ingredients: 114

Pork With Nutmeg Squash Servings: 4 116

Ingredients: 116

Directions: 116

Spiced Broccoli, Cauliflower, And Tofu With Red Onion 118

Ingredients: 118

Directions: 119

Beans And Salmon Pan Servings: 4 120

Ingredients: 120

Directions: 121

Carrot Soup Servings: 4 122

Ingredients: 122

Directions: 123

Healthy Pasta Salad Servings: 6 124

Ingredients: 124

Directions: 124

Chickpea Curry Servings: 4 To 6 126

Ingredients: 126

Directions: 127

Ground Meat Stroganoff Ingredients: 128

Directions: 128

Saucy Short Ribs Servings: 4 130

Ingredients: 130

Directions: 131

Chicken And Gluten-free Noodle Soup Servings: 4 132

Ingredients: 132

Lentil Curry Servings: 4 134

Ingredients: 134

Directions: 135

Chicken And Snap Pea Stir-fry Servings: 4 136

Ingredients: 136

Directions: 137

Juicy Broccolini With Anchovy Almonds Servings: 6 138

Ingredients: 138

Directions: 138

Shiitake And Spinach Pattie Servings: 8 140

Ingredients: 140

Directions: 141

Broccoli Cauliflower Salad Servings: 6 142

Ingredients: 142

Directions: 143

Chicken Salad With Chinese Touch Servings: 3 144

Ingredients: 144

Directions: 145

Amaranth And Quinoa Stuffed Peppers Servings: 4 146

Ingredients: 146

Crispy Cheese-crusted Fish Fillet Servings: 4 148

Ingredients: 148

Directions: 148

Protein Power Beans And Green Stuffed Shells 150

Ingredients: 150

Asian Noodle Salad Ingredients: 153

Directions: 153

Salmon And Green Beans Servings: 4 155

Ingredients: 155

Directions: 155

Cheesy Stuffed Chicken Ingredients: 157

Directions: 158

Arugula With Gorgonzola Dressing Servings: 4 159

Ingredients: 159

Directions: 159

Cabbage Soup Servings: 6 161

Ingredients: 161

Cauliflower Rice Servings: 4 162

Ingredients: 162

Directions: 162

Feta Frittata & Spinach Servings: 4 163

Ingredients: 163

Directions: 163

Fiery Chicken Pot Stickers Ingredients:	165
Directions:	166
Garlic Shrimps With Gritted Cauliflower Servings: 2	167
Ingredients:	167
Directions:	168
Broccoli Tuna Servings: 1	169
Ingredients:	169
Directions:	169
Butternut Squash Soup With Shrimp Servings: 4	170
Ingredients:	170
Directions:	171
Tasty Turkey Baked Balls Servings: 6	172
Ingredients:	172
Directions:	172
Clear Clam Chowder Servings: 4	174
Ingredients:	174
Directions:	175
Rice And Chicken Pot Servings: 4	176
Ingredients:	176
Directions:	177
Sautéed Shrimp Jambalaya Jumble Servings: 4	179
Ingredients:	179
Chicken Chili Servings: 6	181
Ingredients:	181
Directions:	182
Garlic And Lentil Soup Servings: 4	183
Ingredients:	183

Zesty Zucchini & Chicken In Classic Santa Fe Stir-fry 185

Ingredients: 185

Directions: 186

Tilapia Tacos With Awesome Ginger-sesame Slaw 187

Ingredients: 187

Directions: 187

Curry Lentil Stew Servings: 4 189

Ingredients: 189

Directions: 189

Kale Caesar Salad With Grilled Chicken Wrap Servings: 2 191

Ingredients: 191

Directions: 192

Spinach Bean Salad Servings: 1 193

Ingredients: 193

Directions: 193

Crusted Salmon With Walnuts & Rosemary Servings: 6 194

Ingredients: 194

Directions: 195

Baked Sweet Potato With Red Tahini Sauce Servings: 4 196

Ingredients: 196

Directions: 197

Italian Summer Squash Soup Servings: 4 198

Ingredients: 198

Directions: 199

Saffron And Salmon Soup Servings: 4 200

Ingredients: 200

Thai Flavored Hot And Sour Shrimp And Mushroom Soup 202

Ingredients: 202

Directions: 203

Orzo With Sundried Tomatoes Ingredients: 204

Directions: 204

Mushroom And Beet Soup Servings: 4 206

Ingredients: 206

Directions: 206

Chicken Parmesan Meatballs Ingredients: 208

Directions: 208

Meatballs Alla Parmigiana Ingredients: 210

Directions: 211

Sheet Pan Turkey Breast With Golden Vegetables 212

Ingredients: 212

Directions: 212

Coconut Green Curry With Boil Rice Servings: 8 214

Ingredients: 214

Directions: 214

Sweet Potato & Chicken Soup With Lentil Servings: 6 216

Ingredients: 216

Directions: 217

Meatball Taco Bowls Ingredients:

Meatballs:

1 lb. Lean Ground Beef (sub any ground meat like pork, turkey or chicken)

1 Egg

1/4 cup finely cleaved Kale or crisp herbs like Parsley or Cilantro (discretionary)

1 tsp Salt

1/2 tsp Black Pepper

Taco Bowls

2 cups Enchilada Sauce (we utilize custom made) 16 Meatballs (fixings recorded previously)

2 cups Cooked Rice, white or dark colored

1 Avocado, cut

1 cup locally acquired Salsa or Pico de Gallo 1 cup Shredded Cheese

1 Jalapeno, daintily cut (discretionary)

1 Tbsp Cilantro, cleaved

1 Lime, cut into wedges

Tortilla Chips, for serving

Directions:

1. To Make/Freeze

2. In a huge bowl, join ground meat, eggs, kale (if utilizing), salt and pepper. Blend in with your hands just until equitably consolidated.

Structure into 16 meatballs around 1-inch in distance across and place on a sheet dish fixed with foil.

3. In the event that utilizing inside several days, refrigerate for as long as 2 days.

4. In the event that freezing, place sheet container in cooler until meatballs are strong. Move to a cooler sack. Meatballs will keep in the cooler for 3 to 4 months.

5. To Cook

6. In a medium pot, bring enchilada sauce to a low stew. Include meatballs (no compelling reason to defrost first if meatballs were

solidified). Stew meatballs until cooked through, 12 minutes assuming crisp and 20 minutes whenever solidified.

7. While meatballs stew, prep different fixings.

8. Amass taco bowls by garnish rice with meatballs and sauce, cut avocado, salsa, cheddar, jalapeño cuts, and cilantro. Present with lime wedges and tortilla chips.

# Avocado Pesto Zoodles With Salmon *Servings: 4*

Cooking Time: 25 Minutes

Ingredients:

1 tablespoon pesto

1 lemon

2 frozen/fresh salmon steaks

1 large zucchini, spiralized

1 tablespoon black pepper

1 avocado

1/4 cup parmesan, grated

Italian seasoning

Directions:

1. Heat-up the oven to 375 F. Season salmon with Italian seasoning, salt, and pepper and bake for 20 minutes.

2. Add avocados to the bowl along with a tablespoon of pepper, lemon juice, and a tablespoon of pesto. Mash the avocados and keep it aside.

3. Add zucchini noodles to a serving platter, followed by avocado mixture and salmon.

4. Sprinkle with cheese. Add more pesto if needed. Enjoy!

Nutrition Info: 128 calories 9.9 g fat 9 g total carbs 4 g protein

Turmeric-spiced Sweet Potatoes, Apple, And Onion With Chicken

Servings: 4

Cooking Time: 45 Minutes

Ingredients:

2 tablespoons unsalted butter, at room temperature 2 medium sweet potatoes

1 large Granny Smith apple

1 medium onion, thinly sliced

4 bone-in, skin-on chicken breasts

1 teaspoon salt

1 teaspoon turmeric

1 teaspoon dried sage

¼ teaspoon freshly ground black pepper

1 cup apple cider, white wine, or chicken broth Directions:

1. Preheat the oven to 400°F. Grease the baking sheet with the butter.

2. Arrange the sweet potatoes, apple, and onion in a single layer on the baking sheet.

3. Put the chicken, skin-side up, and season with the salt, turmeric, sage, and pepper. Add the cider.

4. Roast within 35 to 40 minutes. Remove, let it rest for 5 minutes and serve.

Nutrition Info: Calories 386 Total Fat: 12g Total Carbohydrates: 26g Sugar: 10g Fiber: 4g Protein: 44g Sodium: 932mg

Seared Herbed Salmon Steak _Servings: 4_

Cooking Time: 5 Minutes

Ingredients:

1 lb. salmon steak, rinsed 1/8 tsp cayenne pepper 1 tsp chili powder

½ tsp cumin

2 garlic cloves, minced

1 tablespoon olive oil

¾ tsp salt

1 tsp freshly ground black pepper

Directions:

1. Preheat the oven to 350 degrees F.

2. In a bowl, combine cayenne pepper, chili powder, cumin, salt, and black pepper. Set aside.

3. Drizzle in olive oil onto the salmon steak. Rub on both sides. Rub garlic and the prepared spice mixture. Let sit for 10 minutes.

4. After allowing the flavors to meld, prepare an ovenproof skillet.

Heat the olive oil. Once hot, season the salmon for 4 minutes on both sides.

5. Transfer skillet inside the oven. Bake for 10 minutes. Serve.

Nutrition Info: Calories 210 Carbs: 0g Fat: 14g Protein: 19g

Tofu And Italian-seasoned Summer Vegetables

Servings: 4

Cooking Time: 20 Minutes

Ingredients:

2 large zucchinis, cut into ¼-inch slices

2 large summer squash, cut into ¼-inch-thick slices 1-pound firm tofu, cut into 1-inch dice

1 cup vegetable broth or water

3 tablespoons extra-virgin olive oil

2 garlic cloves, sliced

1 teaspoon salt

1 teaspoon Italian herb seasoning blend

¼ teaspoon freshly ground black pepper

1 tablespoon thinly sliced fresh basil

Directions:

1. Preheat the oven to 400°F.

2. Combine the zucchini, squash, tofu, broth, oil, garlic, salt, Italian herb seasoning blend, and pepper on a large rimmed baking sheet, and mix well.

3. Roast within 20 minutes.

4. Sprinkle with the basil and serve.

Nutrition Info: Calories 213 Total Fat: 16g Total Carbohydrates: 9g Sugar: 4g Fiber: 3g Protein: 13g Sodium: 806mg

Strawberry And Goat Cheese Salad Ingredients:

1-pound crisp strawberries, diced

Discretionary: 1 to 2 teaspoons nectar or maple syrup, to taste 2 ounces disintegrated goat cheddar (about ½ cup) ¼ cup cleaved crisp basil, in addition to a couple of little basil leaves for embellish

1 tablespoon extra-virgin olive oil

1 tablespoon thick balsamic vinegar*

½ teaspoon Maldon flaky ocean salt or an inadequate ¼

teaspoon fine ocean salt

Crisply ground dark pepper

Directions:

1. Spread the diced strawberries over a medium serving platter or shallow serving bowl. In the event that the strawberries aren't sufficiently sweet exactly as you would prefer, hurl them with a touch of nectar or maple syrup.

2. Sprinkle the disintegrated goat cheddar over the strawberries, trailed by the hacked basil. Shower the olive oil and balsamic vinegar on top.

3. Polish off the plate of mixed greens with the salt, a couple of bits of crisply ground dark pepper, and the saved basil leaves. For the most excellent introduction, serve the plate of mixed greens speedily.

Scraps will keep well in the fridge, however, for around 3 days.

Turmeric Cauliflower And Cod Stew *Servings: 4*

Cooking Time: 30 Minutes

Ingredients:

½ pound cauliflower florets

1-pound cod fillets, boneless, skinless and cubed 1 tablespoons olive oil

1 yellow onion, chopped

½ teaspoon cumin seeds

1 green chili, chopped

¼ teaspoon turmeric powder

2 tomatoes chopped

A pinch of salt and black pepper

½ cup chicken stock

1 tablespoon cilantro, chopped

Directions:

1. Heat up a pot with the oil over medium heat, add the onion, chili, cumin and turmeric, stir and cook for 5 minutes.

2. Add the cauliflower, the fish and the other ingredients, toss, bring to a simmer and cook over medium heat for 25 minutes more.

3. Divide the stew into bowls and serve.

Nutrition Info: calories 281, fat 6, fiber 4, carbs 8, protein 12

Walnuts And Asparagus Delight Servings: 4

Cooking Time: 5 Minutes

Ingredients:

1 and ½ tablespoons olive oil

¾ pound asparagus, trimmed

¼ cup walnuts, chopped

Sunflower seeds and pepper to taste

Directions:

1. Place a skillet over medium heat add olive oil and let it heat up.

2. Add asparagus, Sauté for 5 minutes until browned.

3. Season with sunflower seeds and pepper.

4. Remove heat.

5. Add walnuts and toss.

Nutrition Info: Calories: 124Fat: 12gCarbohydrates: 2gProtein: 3g

Alfredo Zucchini Pasta Ingredients:

2 medium zucchinis spiralized

1-2 TB Vegan Parmesan (discretionary)

Fast Alfredo Sauce

1/2 cup crude cashews drenched for a couple of hours or in bubbling water for 10 minutes

2 TB lemon juice

3 TB nourishing yeast

2 tsp white miso (can sub tamari, soy sauce, or coconut aminos)

1 tsp onion powder

1/2 tsp garlic powder

1/4-1/2 cup water

Directions:

1. Spiralize zucchini noodles.

2. Add all alfredo fixings to a fast blender (beginning with 1/4 cup of water) and mix until smooth. In the event that your sauce is excessively thick,

include more water a tablespoon at once until you get the consistency you're searching for.

3. Top zucchini noodles with alfredo sauce and on the off chance that you'd like, some vegetarian pram.

Quinoa Turkey Chicken Ingredients:

1 cup quinoa, flushed

3-1/2 cups water, isolated

1/2-pound lean ground turkey

1 enormous sweet onion, slashed

1 medium sweet red pepper, slashed

4 garlic cloves, minced

1 tablespoon bean stew powder

1 tablespoon ground cumin

1/2 teaspoon ground cinnamon

2 jars (15 ounces each) dark beans, flushed and depleted 1 can (28 ounces) squashed tomatoes

1 medium zucchini, slashed

1 chipotle pepper in adobo sauce, slashed

1 tablespoon adobo sauce

1 narrows leaf

1 teaspoon dried oregano

1/2 teaspoon salt

1/4 teaspoon pepper

1 cup solidified corn, defrosted

1/4 cup minced crisp cilantro

Discretionary garnishes: Cubed avocado, destroyed Monterey Jack cheddar

Directions:

1. In an enormous pan, heat quinoa and 2 cups water to the point of boiling. Decrease heat; spread and stew for 12-15 minutes or until water is retained. Expel from the warmth; lighten with a fork and put in a safe spot.

2. Then, in an enormous pan covered with cooking shower, cook the turkey, onion, red pepper and garlic over medium warmth until meat is never again pink and vegetables are delicate; channel. Mix in the bean stew powder, cumin and cinnamon; cook 2 minutes longer.

Whenever wanted, present with discretionary garnishes.

3. Include the dark beans, tomatoes, zucchini, chipotle pepper, adobo sauce, sound leaf, oregano, salt, pepper and remaining water.

Heat to the point of boiling. Diminish heat; spread and stew for 30

minutes. Mix in corn and quinoa; heat through. Dispose of narrows leaf; mix in cilantro. Present with discretionary fixings as wanted.

4. Freeze alternative: Freeze cooled stew in cooler compartments.

To utilize, incompletely defrost in fridge medium-term. Warmth through in a pot, blending once in a while; include juices or water if vital.

Garlic & Squash Noodles Servings: 4

Cooking Time: 15 Minutes

Ingredients:

For Preparing Sauce

¼ Cup coconut milk

6 Large dates

2/3g Gritted coconut

6 Garlic cloves

2tbsp Ginger paste

2tbsp Red curry paste

For Preparing Noodles

1 Large boil squash noodles

½ Julienne cut carrots

½ Julienne cut zucchini

1 small red bell pepper

¼ Cup cashew nuts

Directions:

1. For making sauce, blend all the ingredients and make a thick puree.

2. Cut spaghetti squash lengthwise and make noodles.

3. Lightly brush the baking tray with olive oil and bake squash noodles at 40C for 5-6 minutes.

4. For serving, incorporate noodles and puree in a bowl. Or serve puree alongside the noodles.

Nutrition Info: Calories 405 Carbs: 107g Fat: 28g Protein: 7g

Steamed Trout With Red Bean And Chili Salsa

Servings: 1

Cooking Time: 16 Minutes

Ingredients:

4 ½ oz cherry tomatoes, halved

1/4 avocado, unpeeled

6 oz skinless ocean trout fillet

Coriander leaves to serve

2 teaspoons olive oil

Lime wedges, to serve

4 ½ oz canned red kidney beans, rinsed and drained 1/2 red onion, thinly sliced

1 tablespoon pickled jalapenos, drained

1/2 teaspoon ground cumin

4 Sicilian olives/green olives

Directions:

1. Put a steamer basket over a pot of simmering water. Add fish to the basket and cover, cook for 10-12 minutes.

2. Remove the fish, then let it rest for a few minutes. In the meantime, preheat some oil in a pan.

3. Add pickled jalapenos, red kidney beans, olives, 1/2 teaspoon cumin, and cherry tomatoes. Cook for about 4-5 minutes, stirring continuously.

4. Scoop the bean batter onto a serving platter, followed by trout.

Add coriander and onion on top.

5. Serve along with lime wedges and avocado. Enjoy steamed ocean trout with red bean and chili salsa!

Nutrition Info: 243 calories 33.2 g fat 18.8 g total carbs 44 g protein

Sweet Potato And Turkey Soup _Servings: 4_

Cooking Time: 45 Minutes

Ingredients:

2 tablespoons olive oil

1 yellow onion, chopped

1 green bell pepper, chopped

2 sweet potatoes, peeled and cubed

1-pound turkey breast, skinless, boneless and cubed 1 teaspoon coriander, ground

A pinch of salt and black pepper

1 teaspoon sweet paprika

6 cups chicken stock

Juice of 1 lime

A handful parsley, chopped

Directions:

1. Heat up a pot with the oil over medium heat, add the onion, the bell pepper and the sweet potatoes, stir and cook for 5 minutes.

2. Add the meat and brown for 5 minutes more.

3. Add the rest of the ingredients, toss, bring to a simmer and cook over medium heat for 35 minutes more.

4. Ladle the soup into bowls and serve.

Nutrition Info: calories 203, fat 5, fiber 4, carbs 7, protein 8

Miso Broiled Salmon Servings: 2

Cooking Time: 20 Minutes

Ingredients:

2 tbsp. Maple Syrup

2 Lemons

¼ cup Miso

¼ tsp. Pepper, grounded

2 Limes

2 ½ lb. Salmon, skin-on

Dash of Cayenne Pepper

2 tbsp. Extra Virgin Olive Oil

¼ cup Miso

Directions:

1. First, mix the lime juice and lemon juice in a small bowl until combined well.

2. Next, spoon in the miso, cayenne pepper, maple syrup, olive oil, and pepper to it. Combine well.

3. Then, place the salmon on a parchment paper-lined baking sheet with the skin side down.

4. Brush the salmon generously with the miso lemon mixture.

5. Now, place the halved lemon and lime pieces on the sides with the cut side up.

6. Finally, bake them for 8 to 12 minutes or until the fish flakes.

Nutrition Info: Calories: 230KcalProteins: 28.3gCarbohydrates: 6.7gFat: 8.7g

Simply Sautéed Flaky Fillet Servings: 6

Cooking Time: 8 Minutes

Ingredients:

6-fillets tilapia

2-Tbsp.s olive oil

1-pc lemon, juice

Salt and pepper to taste

¼-cup parsley or cilantro, chopped

Directions:

1. Sauté tilapia fillets with olive oil in a medium-sized skillet placed over medium heat. Cook for 4 minutes on each side until the fish flakes easily with a fork.

2. Add salt and pepper to taste. Pour the lemon juice to each fillet.

3. To serve, sprinkle the cooked fillets with chopped parsley or cilantro.

Nutrition Info: Calories: 249 CalFat: 8.3 g Protein: 18.6 g Carbs: 25.9

Fiber: 1 g

Pork Carnitas _Servings: 10_

Cooking Time: 8 Hrs. 10 Minutes

Ingredients:

5 lbs. pork shoulder

2 garlic cloves, minced

1 tsp black pepper

1/4 tsp cinnamon

1 tsp dried oregano

1 tsp ground cumin

1 bay leaf

2 oz chicken broth

1 tsp lime juice

1 tbsp chili powder

1 tbsp salt

Directions:

1. Add pork along with the rest of the ingredients in a Slow Cooker.

2. Put on its lid and cook for 8 hrs. on low heat.

3. Once done, shred the cooked pork using a fork.

4. Spread this shredded pork on a baking tray.

5. Broil for 10 minutes then serve.

Nutrition Info: Calories 547 Fat 39 g, Carbs 2.6 g, Fiber 0 g, Protein 43 g

White Fish Chowder With Vegetables

Servings: 6 To 8

Cooking Time: 32 To 35 Minutes

Ingredients:

3 sweet potatoes, peeled and cut into ½-inch pieces 4 carrots, peeled and cut into ½-inch pieces 3 cups full-fat coconut milk

2 cups water

1 teaspoon dried thyme

½ teaspoon sea salt

10½ ounces (298 g) white fish, skinless and firm, such as cod or halibut, cut into chunks

Directions:

1. Add the sweet potatoes, carrots, coconut milk, water, thyme, and sea salt to a large saucepan over high heat, and bring to a boil.

2. Reduce the heat to low, cover, and simmer for 20 minutes until the vegetables are tender, stirring occasionally.

3. Pour half of the soup to a blender and purée until thoroughly mixed and smooth, then return it to the pot.

4. Stir in the fish chunks and continue cooking for an additional 12 to 15 minutes, or until the fish is cooked through.

5. Remove from the heat and serve in bowls.

Nutrition Info: calories: 450 ; fat: 28.7g ; protein: 14.2g ; carbs: 38.8g ; fiber: 8.1g ; sugar: 6.7g; sodium: 250mg

Lemony Mussels _Servings: 4_

Ingredients:

1 tbsp. extra virgin extra virgin olive oil 2 minced garlic cloves

2 lbs. scrubbed mussels

Juice of one lemon

Directions:

1. Put some water in a pot, add mussels, bring with a boil over medium heat, cook for 5 minutes, discard unopened mussels and transfer them with a bowl.

2. In another bowl, mix the oil with garlic and freshly squeezed lemon juice, whisk well, and add over the mussels, toss and serve.

3. Enjoy!

Nutrition Info: Calories: 140, Fat:4 g, Carbs:8 g, Protein:8 g, Sugars: 4g, Sodium:600 mg,

Lime & Chili Salmon _Servings: 2_

Cooking Time: 8 Minutes

Ingredients:

1 lb. salmon

1 tablespoon lime juice

½ teaspoon pepper

½ teaspoon chili powder

4 lime slices

Directions:

1. Drizzle salmon with lime juice.

2. Sprinkle both sides with pepper and chili powder.

3. Add salmon to the air fryer.

4. Place lime slices on top of salmon.

5. Air fry at 375 degrees F for 8 minutes.

Cheesy Tuna Pasta _Servings: 3-4_

Ingredients:

2 c. arugula

¼ c. chopped green onions

1 tbs. red vinegar

5 oz. drained canned tuna

¼ tsp. black pepper

2 oz. cooked whole-wheat pasta

1 tbsp. olive oil

1 tbsp. grated low-fat parmesan

Directions:

1. Cook the pasta in unsalted water until ready. Drain and set aside.

2. In a bowl of large size, thoroughly mix the tuna, green onions, vinegar, oil, arugula, pasta, and black pepper.

3. Toss well and top with the cheese.

4. Serve and enjoy.

Nutrition Info: Calories: 566.3, Fat:42.4 g, Carbs:18.6 g, Protein:29.8 g, Sugars:0.4 g, Sodium:688.6 mg

Coconut Crusted Fish Strips _Servings: 4_

Cooking Time: 12 Minutes

Ingredients:

Marinade

1 tablespoon soy sauce

1 teaspoon ground ginger

½ cup coconut milk

2 tablespoons maple syrup

½ cup pineapple juice

2 teaspoons hot sauce

Fish

1 lb. fish fillet, sliced into strips

Pepper to taste

1 cup breadcrumbs

1 cup coconut flakes (unsweetened)

Cooking spray

Directions:

1. Mix marinade ingredients in a bowl.

2. Stir in fish strips.

3. Cover and refrigerate for 2 hours.

4. Preheat your air fryer to 375 degrees F.

5. In a bowl, mix pepper, breadcrumbs and coconut flakes.

6. Dip fish strips in the breadcrumb mixture.

7. Spray your air fryer basket with oil.

8. Add fish strips to the air fryer basket.

9. Air fry for 6 minutes per side.

Mexican Fish _Servings: 2_

Cooking Time: 10 Minutes

Ingredients:

4 fish fillets

2 teaspoons Mexican oregano

4 teaspoons cumin

4 teaspoons chili powder

Pepper to taste

Cooking spray

Directions:

1. Preheat your air fryer to 400 degrees F.

2. Spray fish with oil.

3. Season both sides of fish with spices and pepper.

4. Place fish in the air fryer basket.

5. Cook for 5 minutes.

6. Flip and cook for another 5 minutes.

Trout With Cucumber Salsa *Servings: 4*

Cooking Time: 10 Minutes

Ingredients:

Salsa:

1 English cucumber, diced

¼ cup unsweetened coconut yogurt

2 tablespoons chopped fresh mint

1 scallion, white and green parts, chopped

1 teaspoon raw honey

Sea salt

Fish:

4 (5-ounce) trout fillets, patted dry

1 tablespoon olive oil

Sea salt and freshly ground black pepper, to taste Directions:

1. Make the salsa: Stir together the yogurt, cucumber, mint, scallion, honey, and sea salt in a small bowl until completely mixed. Set aside.

2. On a clean work surface, rub the trout fillets lightly with sea salt and pepper.

3. Heat the olive oil in a large skillet over medium heat. Add the trout fillets to the hot skillet and panfry for about 10 minutes, flipping the fish halfway through, or until the fish is cooked to your liking.

4. Spread the salsa on top of the fish and serve.

Nutrition Info: calories: 328 ; fat: 16.2g ; protein: 38.9g ; carbs: 6.1g

; fiber: 1.0g ; sugar: 3.2g; sodium: 477mg

Lemon Zoodles With Shrimp Servings: 4

Cooking Time: 0 Minutes

Ingredients:

Sauce:

½ cup packed fresh basil leaves

Juice of 1 lemon (or 3 tablespoons)

1 teaspoon bottled minced garlic

Pinch sea salt

Pinch freshly ground black pepper

¼ cup canned full-fat coconut milk

1 large yellow squash, julienned or spiralized 1 large zucchini, julienned or spiralized

1 pound (454 g) shrimp, deveined, boiled, peeled, and chilled Zest of 1 lemon (optional)

Directions:

1. Make the sauce: Process the basil leaves, lemon juice, garlic, sea salt, and pepper in a food processor until chopped thoroughly.

2. Slowly pour in the coconut milk while the processor is still running. Pulse until smooth.

3. Transfer the sauce to a large bowl, along with the yellow squash and zucchini. Toss well.

4. Scatter the shrimp and lemon zest (if desired) on top of the noodles. Serve immediately.

Nutrition Info: calories: 246 ; fat: 13.1g ; protein: 28.2g ; carbs: 4.9g

; fiber: 2.0g ; sugar: 2.8g; sodium: 139mg

Crispy Shrimp Servings: 4

Cooking Time: 3 Minutes

Ingredients:

1 lb. shrimp, peeled and deveined

½ cup fish breading mix

Cooking spray

Directions:

1. Preheat your air fryer to 390 degrees F.

2. Spray shrimp with oil.

3. Coat with the breading mix.

4. Spray air fryer basket with oil.

5. Add shrimp to air fryer basket.

6. Cook for 3 minutes.

Broiled Sea Bass _Servings: 2_

Ingredients:

2 minced garlic cloves

Pepper.

1 tbsp. lemon juice

2 white sea bass fillets

¼ tsp. herb seasoning blend

Directions:

1. Spray a broiler pan with some olive oil and place the fillets on it.

2. Sprinkle the lemon juice, garlic and the spices over the fillets.

3. Broil for about 10 min or until the fish is golden.

4. Serve over a bed of sautéed spinach if desired.

Nutrition Info: Calories: 169, Fat:9.3 g, Carbs:0.34 g, Protein:15.3 g, Sugars:0.2 g, Sodium:323 mg

Salmon Cakes _Servings: 4_

Cooking Time: 10 Minutes

Ingredients:

Cooking spray

1 lb. salmon fillet, flaked

¼ cup almond flour

2 teaspoons Old Bay seasoning

1 green onion, chopped

Directions:

1. Preheat your air fryer to 390 degrees F.

2. Spray your air fryer basket with oil.

3. In a bowl, combine the remaining ingredients.

4. Form patties from the mixture.

5. Spray both sides of patties with oil.

6. Air fry for 8 minutes.

Spicy Cod _Servings: 4_

Ingredients:

2 tbsps. Fresh chopped parsley

2 lbs. cod fillets

2 c. low sodium salsa

1 tbsp. flavorless oil

Directions:

1. Preheat the oven to 350°F.

2. In a large, deep baking dish drizzle the oil along the bottom.

Place the cod fillets in the dish. Pour the salsa over the fish. Cover with foil for 20 minutes. Remove the foil last 10 minutes of cooking.

3. Bake in the oven for 20 – 30 minutes, until the fish is flaky.

4. Serve with white or brown rice. Garnish with parsley.

Nutrition Info: Calories: 110, Fat:11 g, Carbs:83 g, Protein:16.5 g, Sugars:0 g, Sodium:122 mg

Smoked Trout Spread Servings: 2

Ingredients:

2 tsps. Fresh lemon juice

½ c. low-fat cottage cheese

1 diced celery stalk

¼ lb. skinned smoked trout fillet,

½ tsp. Worcestershire sauce

1 tsp. hot pepper sauce

¼ c. coarsely chopped red onion

Directions:

1. Combine the trout, cottage cheese, red onion, lemon juice, hot pepper sauce and Worcestershire sauce in a blender or food processor.

2. Process until smooth, stopping to scrape down the sides of the bowl as needed.

3. Fold in the diced celery.

4. Keep in an air-tight container in the refrigerator.

Nutrition Info: Calories: 57, Fat:4 g, Carbs:1 g, Protein:4 g, Sugars:0 g, Sodium:660 mg

Tuna And Shallots _Servings: 4_

Ingredients:

½ c. low-sodium chicken stock

1 tbsp. olive oil

4 boneless and skinless tuna fillets

2 chopped shallots

1 tsp. sweet paprika

2 tbsps. lime juice

¼ tsp. black pepper

Directions:

1. Heat up a pan with the oil over medium-high heat, add shallots and sauté for 3 minutes.

2. Add the fish and cook it for 4 minutes on each side.

3. Add the rest of the ingredients, cook everything for 3 minutes more, divide between plates and serve.

Nutrition Info: Calories: 4040, Fat:34.6 g, Carbs:3 g, Protein:21.4 g, Sugars:0.5 g, Sodium:1000 mg

Lemon Pepper Shrimp *Servings: 2*

Cooking Time: 10 Minutes

Ingredients:

1 tablespoon lemon juice

1 tablespoon olive oil

1 teaspoon lemon pepper

¼ teaspoon garlic powder

¼ teaspoon paprika

12 oz. shrimp, peeled and deveined

Directions:

1. Preheat your air fryer to 400 degrees F.

2. Mix lemon juice, olive oil, lemon pepper, garlic powder and paprika in a bowl.

3. Stir in shrimp and coat evenly with the mixture.

4. Add to the air fryer.

5. Cook for 8 minutes.

Hot Tuna Steak _Servings: 6_

Ingredients:

2 tbsps. Fresh lemon juice

Pepper.

Roasted orange garlic mayonnaise

¼ c. whole black peppercorns

6 sliced tuna steaks

2 tbsps. Extra-virgin olive oil

Salt

Directions:

1. Place the tuna in a bowl to fit. Add the oil, lemon juice, salt and pepper. Turn the tuna to coat well in the marinade. Let rest 15 to 20

minutes, turning once.

2. Place the peppercorns in a double thickness of plastic bags. Tap the peppercorns with a heavy saucepan or small mallet to crush them coarsely. Place on a large plate.

3. When ready to cook the tuna, dip the edges into the crushed peppercorns. Heat a nonstick skillet over medium heat. Sear the tuna steaks, in batches if necessary, for 4 minutes per side for medium-rare fish, adding 2 to 3 tablespoons of the marinade to the skillet if necessary, to prevent sticking.

4. Serve dolloped with roasted orange garlic mayonnaise <u>Nutrition Info:</u> Calories: 124, Fat:0.4 g, Carbs:0.6 g, Protein:28 g, Sugars:0 g, Sodium:77 mg

Cajun Salmon _Servings: 2_

Cooking Time: 10 Minutes

Ingredients:

2 salmon fillets

Cooking spray

1 tablespoon Cajun seasoning

1 tablespoon honey

Directions:

1. Preheat your air fryer to 390 degrees F.

2. Spray both sides of fish with oil.

3. Sprinkle with Cajun seasoning.

4. Spray air fryer basket with oil.

5. Add salmon to the air fryer basket.

6. Air fry for 10 minutes.

Quinoa Salmon Bowl With Vegetables

Servings: 4

Cooking Time: 0 Minutes

Ingredients:

1 pound (454 g) cooked salmon, flaked

4 cups cooked quinoa

6 radishes, thinly sliced

1 zucchini, sliced into half moons

3 cups arugula

3 scallions, minced

½ cup almond oil

1 teaspoon sugar-free hot sauce

1 tablespoon apple cider vinegar

1 teaspoon sea salt

½ cup toasted slivered almonds, for garnish (optional) <u>Directions:</u>

1. In a large bowl, mix together the flaked salmon, cooked quinoa, radishes, zucchini, arugula, and scallions, and stir well.

2. Fold in the almond oil, hot sauce, apple cider vinegar, and sea salt and toss to combine.

3. Divide the mixture into four bowls. Scatter each bowl evenly with the slivered almonds for garnish, if desired. Serve immediately.

Nutrition Info: calories: 769 ; fat: 51.6g ; protein: 37.2g ; carbs: 44.8g ; fiber: 8.0g ; sugar: 4.0g; sodium: 681mg

Crumbed Fish Servings: 4

Cooking Time: 15 Minutes

Ingredients:

¼ cup olive oil

1 cup dry breadcrumbs

4 white fish fillets

Pepper to taste

Directions:

1. Preheat your air fryer to 350 degrees F.

2. Sprinkle both sides of fish with pepper.

3. Combine oil and breadcrumbs in a bowl.

4. Dip the fish into the mixture.

5. Press breadcrumbs to adhere.

6. Place fish in the air fryer.

7. Cook for 15 minutes.

Simple Salmon Patties Servings: 4

Cooking Time: 8 To 10 Minutes

Ingredients:

1 pound (454 g) skinless boned salmon fillets, minced ¼ cup minced sweet onion

½ cup almond flour

2 garlic cloves, minced

2 eggs, whisked

1 teaspoon Dijon mustard

1 tablespoon freshly squeezed lemon juice

Dash red pepper flakes

½ teaspoon sea salt

¼ teaspoon freshly ground black pepper

1 tablespoon avocado oil

Directions:

1. Mix together the minced salmon, sweet onion, almond flour, garlic, whisked eggs, mustard, lemon juice, red pepper flakes, sea salt, and pepper in a large bowl, and stir until well incorporated.

2. Allow the salmon mixture to rest for 5 minutes.

3. Scoop out the salmon mixture and shape into four ½-inch-thick patties with your hands.

4. Heat the avocado oil in a large skillet over medium heat. Add the patties to the hot skillet and cook each side for 4 to 5 minutes until lightly browned and cooked through.

5. Remove from the heat and serve on a plate.

Nutrition Info: calories: 248 ; fat: 13.4g ; protein: 28.4g ; carbs: 4.1g ; fiber: 2.0g ; sugar: 2.0g; sodium: 443mg

Popcorn Shrimp Servings: 4

Cooking Time: 10 Minutes

Ingredients:

½ teaspoon onion powder

½ teaspoon garlic powder

½ teaspoon paprika

¼ teaspoon ground mustard

⅛ teaspoon dried sage

⅛ teaspoon ground thyme

⅛ teaspoon dried oregano

⅛ teaspoon dried basil

Pepper to taste

3 tablespoons cornstarch

1 lb. shrimp, peeled and deveined

Cooking spray

Directions:

1. Combine all ingredients except shrimp in a bowl.

2. Coat shrimp with the mixture.

3. Spray air fryer basket with oil.

4. Preheat your air fryer to 390 degrees F.

5. Add shrimp inside.

6. Air fry for 4 minutes.

7. Shake the basket.

8. Cook for another 5 minutes.

Spicy Baked Fish _Servings: 5_

Ingredients:

1 tbsp. olive oil

1 tsp. spice salt free seasoning

1 lb. salmon fillet

Directions:

1. Preheat the oven to 350F.

2. Sprinkle the fish with olive oil and the seasoning.

3. Bake for 15 min uncovered.

4. Slice and serve.

Nutrition Info: Calories: 192, Fat:11 g, Carbs:14.9 g, Protein:33.1 g, Sugars:0.3 g, Sodium:505 6 mg

Paprika Tuna Servings: 4

Ingredients:

½ tsp. chili powder

2 tsps. sweet paprika

¼ tsp. black pepper

2 tbsps. olive oil

4 boneless tuna steaks

Directions:

1. Heat up a pan with the oil over medium-high heat, add the tuna steaks, season with paprika, black pepper and chili powder, cook for 5 minutes on each side, divide between plates and serve with a side salad.

Nutrition Info: Calories: 455, Fat:20.6 g, Carbs:0.8 g, Protein:63.8 g, Sugars:7.4 g, Sodium: 411 mg

Fish Patties Servings: 2

Cooking Time: 7 Minutes

Ingredients:

8 oz. white fish fillet, flaked

Garlic powder to taste

1 teaspoon lemon juice

Directions:

1. Preheat your air fryer to 390 degrees F.

2. Combine all the ingredients.

3. Form patties from the mixture.

4. Place fish patties in the air fryer.

5. Cook for 7 minutes.

Seared Scallops With Honey Servings: 4

Cooking Time: 15 Minutes

Ingredients:

1 pound (454 g) large scallops, rinsed and patted dry Dash sea salt

Dash freshly ground black pepper

2 tablespoons avocado oil

¼ cup raw honey

3 tablespoons coconut aminos

1 tablespoon apple cider vinegar

2 garlic cloves, minced

Directions:

1. In a bowl, add the scallops, sea salt, and pepper and toss until coated well.

2. In a large skillet, heat the avocado oil over medium-high heat.

3. Sear the scallops for 2 to 3 minutes on each side, or until the scallops turn milky white or opaque and firm.

4. Remove the scallops from the heat to a plate and loosely tent with foil to keep warm. Set aside.

5. Add the honey, coconut aminos, vinegar, and garlic to the skillet and stir well.

6. Bring to a simmer and cook for about 7 minutes until the liquid is reduced, stirring occasionally.

7. Return the seared scallops to the skillet, stirring to coat them with the glaze.

8. Divide the scallops among four plates and serve warm.

Nutrition Info: calories: 382 ; fat: 18.9g ; protein: 21.2g ; carbs: 26.1g ; fiber: 1.0g ; sugar: 17.7g; sodium: 496mg

Cod Fillets With Shiitake Mushrooms Servings: 4

Cooking Time: 15 To 18 Minutes

Ingredients:

1 garlic clove, minced

1 leek, thinly sliced

1 teaspoon minced fresh ginger root

1 tablespoon olive oil

½ cup dry white wine

½ cup sliced shiitake mushrooms

4 (6-ounce / 170-g) cod fillets

1 teaspoon sea salt

⅛ teaspoon freshly ground black pepper

Directions:

1. Preheat the oven to 375ºF (190ºC).

2. Mix together the garlic, leek, ginger root, wine, olive oil, and mushrooms in a baking pan, and toss until the mushrooms are evenly coated.

3. Bake in the preheated oven for 10 minutes until lightly browned.

4. Remove the baking pan from the oven. Spread the cod fillets on top and season with sea salt and pepper.

5. Cover with aluminum foil and return to the oven. Bake for 5 to 8 minutes more, or until the fish is flaky.

6. Remove the aluminum foil and cool for 5 minutes before serving.

Nutrition Info: calories: 166 ; fat: 6.9g ; protein: 21.2g ; carbs: 4.8g ; fiber: 1.0g ; sugar: 1.0g; sodium: 857mg

Broiled White Sea Bass _Servings: 2_

Ingredients:

1 tsp. minced garlic

Ground black pepper

1 tbsp. lemon juice

8 oz. white sea bass fillets

¼ tsp. salt-free herbed seasoning blend

Directions:

1. Preheat the broiler and position the rack 4 inches from the heat source.

2. Lightly spray a baking pan with cooking spray. Place the fillets in the pan. Sprinkle the lemon juice, garlic, herbed seasoning and pepper over the fillets.

3. Broil until the fish is opaque throughout when tested with a tip of a knife, about 8 to 10 minutes.

4. Serve immediately.

Nutrition Info: Calories: 114, Fat:2 g, Carbs:2 g, Protein:21 g, Sugars:0.5 g, Sodium:78 mg

Baked Tomato Hake Servings: 4-5

Ingredients:

½ c. tomato sauce

1 tbsp. olive oil

Parsley

2 sliced tomatoes

½ c. grated cheese

4 lbs. de-boned and sliced hake fish

Salt.

Directions:

1. Preheat the oven to 400 0F.

2. Season the fish with salt.

3. In a skillet or saucepan; stir-fry the fish in the olive oil until half-done.

4. Take four foil papers to cover the fish.

5. Shape the foil to resemble containers; add the tomato sauce into each foil container.

6. Add the fish, tomato slices, and top with grated cheese.

7. Bake until you get a golden crust, for approximately 20-25 minutes.

8. Open the packs and top with parsley.

<u>Nutrition Info:</u> Calories: 265, Fat:15 g, Carbs:18 g, Protein:22 g, Sugars:0.5 g, Sodium:94.6 mg

Seared Haddock With Beets Servings: 4

Cooking Time: 30 Minutes

Ingredients:

8 beets, peeled and cut into eighths

2 shallots, thinly sliced

2 tablespoons apple cider vinegar

2 tablespoons olive oil, divided

1 teaspoon bottled minced garlic

1 teaspoon chopped fresh thyme

Pinch sea salt

4 (5-ounce / 142-g) haddock fillets, patted dry <u>Directions:</u>

1. Preheat the oven to 400ºF (205ºC).

2. Combine the beets, shallots, vinegar, 1 tablespoon of olive oil, garlic, thyme, and sea salt in a medium bowl, and toss to coat well.

Spread out the beet mixture in a baking dish.

3. Roast in the preheated oven for about 30 minutes, turning once or twice with a spatula, or until the beets are tender.

4. Meanwhile, heat the remaining 1 tablespoon of olive oil in a large skillet over medium-high heat.

5. Add the haddock and sear each side for 4 to 5 minutes, or until the flesh is opaque and it flakes apart easily.

6. Transfer the fish to a plate and serve topped with the roasted beets.

Nutrition Info: calories: 343 ; fat: 8.8g ; protein: 38.1g ; carbs: 20.9g

; fiber: 4.0g ; sugar: 11.5g; sodium: 540mg

Heartfelt Tuna Melt Servings: 4

Ingredients:

3 oz. grated reduced-fat cheddar cheese

1/3 c. chopped celery

Black pepper and salt

¼ c. chopped onion

2 whole-wheat English muffins

6 oz. drained white tuna

¼ c. low fat Russian

Directions:

1. Preheat broiler. Combine tuna, celery, onion and salad dressing.

2. Season with salt and pepper.

3. Toast English muffin halves.

4. Place split-side-up on baking sheet and top each with 1/4 of tuna mixture.

5. Broil 2-3 minutes or until heated through.

6. Top with cheese and return to broiler until cheese is melted, about 1 minute longer.

Nutrition Info: Calories: 320, Fat:16.7 g, Carbs:17.1 g, Protein:25.7 g, Sugars:5.85 g, Sodium:832 mg

Lemon Salmon With Kaffir Lime Servings: 8

Ingredients:

1 quartered and bruised lemon grass stalk

2 kaffir torn lime leaves

1 thinly sliced lemon

1 ½ c. fresh coriander leaves

1 whole side salmon fillet

Directions:

1. Pre-heat the oven to 350°F.

2. Cover a baking pan with foil sheets, overlapping the sides 3. Place the Salmon on the foil, top with the lemon, lime leaves, the lemon grass and 1 cup of the coriander leaves. Option: season with salt and pepper.

4. Bring the long side of the foil to the center before folding the seal.

Roll the ends in order to close up the salmon.

5. Bake for 30 minutes.

6. Transfer the cooked fish to a platter. Top with fresh coriander.

Serve with white or brown rice.

Nutrition Info: Calories: 103, Fat:11.8 g, Carbs:43.5 g, Protein:18 g, Sugars:0.7 g, Sodium:322 mg

Tender Salmon In Mustard Sauce Servings: 2

Ingredients:

5 tbsps. Minced dill

2/3 c. sour cream

Pepper.

2 tbsps. Dijon mustard

1 tsp. garlic powder

5 oz. salmon fillets

2-3 tbsps. Lemon juice

Directions:

1. Mix sour cream, mustard, lemon juice and dill.

2. Season the fillets with pepper and garlic powder.

3. Arrange the salmon on a baking sheet skin side down and cover with the prepared mustard sauce.

4. Bake for 20 minutes at 390°F.

Nutrition Info: Calories: 318, Fat:12 g, Carbs:8 g, Protein:40.9 g, Sugars:909.4 g, Sodium:1.4 mg

Crab Salad _Servings: 4_

Ingredients:

2 c. crab meat

1 c. halved cherry tomatoes

1 tbsp. olive oil

Black pepper

1 chopped shallot

1/3 c. chopped cilantro

1 tbsp. lemon juice

Directions:

1. In a bowl, combine the crab with the tomatoes and the other ingredients, toss and serve.

Nutrition Info: Calories: 54, Fat:3.9 g, Carbs:2.6 g, Protein:2.3 g, Sugars:2.3 g, Sodium:462.5 mg

Baked Salmon With Miso Sauce Servings: 4

Cooking Time: 15 To 20 Minutes

Ingredients:

Sauce:

¼ cup apple cider

¼ cup white miso

1 tablespoon olive oil

1 tablespoon white rice vinegar

⅛ teaspoon ground ginger

4 (3- to 4-ounce / 85- to 113-g) boneless salmon fillets 1 sliced scallion, for garnish

⅛ teaspoon red pepper flakes, for garnish

Directions:

1. Preheat the oven to 375ºF (190ºC).

2. Make the sauce: Whisk together the apple cider, white miso, olive oil, rice vinegar, ginger in a small bowl. Add a little water if a thinner consistency is desired.

3. Arrange the salmon fillets in a baking pan, skin-side down. Spoon the prepared sauce over the fillets to coat evenly.

4. Bake in the preheated oven for 15 to 20 minutes, or until the fish flakes easily with a fork.

5. Garnish with the sliced scallion and red pepper flakes and serve.

Nutrition Info: calories: 466 ; fat: 18.4g ; protein: 67.5g ; carbs: 9.1g ; fiber: 1.0g ; sugar: 2.7g; sodium: 819mg

Herb-coated Baked Cod With Honey Servings: 2

Ingredients:

6 tbsps. Herb-flavored stuffing

8 oz. cod fillets

2 tbsps. Honey

Directions:

1. Preheat your oven to 375 0F.

2. Spray a baking pan lightly with cooking spray.

3. Put the herb-flavored stuffing in a bag and close. Squash the stuffing until it gets crumbly.

4. Coat the fishes with honey and get rid of the remaining honey.

Add one fillet to the bag of stuffing and shake gently to coat the fish completely.

5. Transfer the cod to the baking pan and repeat the process for the second fish.

6. Wrap the fillets with foil and bake until firm and opaque all through when you test with the tip of a knife blade, about ten minutes.

7. Serve hot.

<u>Nutrition Info:</u> Calories: 185, Fat:1 g, Carbs:23 g, Protein:21 g, Sugars:2 g, Sodium:144.3 mg

Parmesan Cod Mix *Servings: 4*

Ingredients:

1 tbsp. lemon juice

½ c. chopped green onion

4 boneless cod fillets

3 minced garlic cloves

1 tbsp. olive oil

½ c. shredded low-fat parmesan cheese

Directions:

1. Heat up a pan with the oil over medium heat, add the garlic and the green onions, toss and sauté for 5 minutes.

2. Add the fish and cook it for 4 minutes on each side.

3. Add the lemon juice, sprinkle the parmesan on top, cook everything for 2 minutes more, divide between plates and serve.

Nutrition Info: Calories: 275, Fat:22.1 g, Carbs:18.2 g, Protein:12 g, Sugars:0.34 g, Sodium:285.4 mg

Crispy Garlic Shrimp Servings: 4

Cooking Time: 10 Minutes

Ingredients:

1 lb. shrimp, peeled and deveined

2 teaspoons garlic powder

Pepper to taste

¼ cup flour

Cooking spray

Directions:

1. Season shrimp with garlic powder and pepper.

2. Coat with flour.

3. Spray your air fryer basket with oil.

4. Add shrimp to the air fryer basket.

5. Cook at 400 degrees F for 10 minutes, shaking once halfway through.

Creamy Sea Bass Mix *Servings: 4*

Ingredients:

1 tbsp. chopped parsley

2 tbsps. avocado oil

1 c. coconut cream

1 tbsp. lime juice

1 chopped yellow onion

¼ tsp. black pepper

4 boneless sea bass fillets

Directions:

1. Heat up a pan with the oil over medium heat, add the onion, toss and sauté for 2 minutes.

2. Add the fish and cook it for 4 minutes on each side.

3. Add the rest of the ingredients, cook everything for 4 minutes more, divide between plates and serve.

Nutrition Info: Calories: 283, Fat:12.3 g, Carbs:12.5 g, Protein:8 g, Sugars:6 g, Sodium:508.8 mg

Cucumber Ahi Poke *Servings: 4*

Cooking Time: 0 Minutes

Ingredients:

Ahi Poke:

1 pound (454 g) sushi-grade ahi tuna, cut into 1-inch cubes 3 tablespoons coconut aminos

3 scallions, thinly sliced

1 serrano chile, deseeded and minced (optional) 1 teaspoon olive oil

1 teaspoon rice vinegar

1 teaspoon toasted sesame seeds

Dash ground ginger

1 large avocado, diced

1 cucumber, sliced into ½-inch-thick rounds Directions:

1. Make the ahi poke: Toss the ahi tuna cubes with the coconut aminos, scallions, serrano chile (if desired), olive oil, vinegar, sesame seeds, and ginger in a large bowl.

2. Cover the bowl with plastic wrap and marinate in the fridge for 15

minutes.

3. Add the diced avocado to the bowl of ahi poke and stir to incorporate.

4. Arrange the cucumber rounds on a serving plate. Spoon the ahi poke over the cucumber and serve.

Nutrition Info: calories: 213 ; fat: 15.1g ; protein: 10.1g ; carbs: 10.8g ; fiber: 4.0g ; sugar: 0.6g; sodium: 70mg

Minty Cod Mix Servings: 4

Ingredients:

4 boneless cod fillets

½ c. low-sodium chicken stock

2 tbsps. olive oil

¼ tsp. black pepper

1 tbsp. chopped mint

1 tsps. grated lemon zest

¼ c. chopped shallot

1 tbsp. lemon juice

Directions:

1. Heat up a pan with the oil over medium heat, add the shallots, stir and sauté for 5 minutes.

2. Add the cod, the lemon juice and the other ingredients, bring to a simmer and cook over medium heat for 12 minutes.

3. Divide everything between plates and serve.

<u>Nutrition Info:</u> Calories: 160, Fat:8.1 g, Carbs:2 g, Protein:20.5 g, Sugars:8 g, Sodium:45 mg

Lemony & Creamy Tilapia _Servings: 4_

Ingredients:

2 tbsps. Chopped fresh cilantro

¼ c. low-fat mayonnaise

Freshly ground black pepper

¼ c. fresh lemon juice

4 tilapia fillets

½ c. grated low-fat parmesan cheese

½ tsp. garlic powder

Directions:

1. In a bowl, mix together all ingredients except tilapia fillets and cilantro.

2. Coat the fillets with mayonnaise mixture evenly.

3. Place the filets onto a large foil paper. Wrap the foil paper around fillets to seal them.

4. Arrange the foil packet in the bottom of a large slow cooker.

5. Set the slow cooker on low.

6. Cover and cook for 3-4 hours.

7. Serve with the garnishing of cilantro.

Nutrition Info: Calories: 133.6, Fat:2.4 g, Carbs:4.6 g, Protein:22 g, Sugars:0.9 g, Sodium:510.4 mg

Fish Tacos Servings: 4

Cooking Time: 20 Minutes

Ingredients:

Cooking spray

1 tablespoon olive oil

4 cups cabbage slaw

1 tablespoon apple cider vinegar

1 tablespoon lime juice

Pinch cayenne pepper

Pepper to taste

2 tablespoons taco seasoning mix

¼ cup all-purpose flour

1 lb. cod fillet, sliced into cubes

4 corn tortillas

Directions:

1. Preheat your air fryer to 400 degrees F.

2. Spray your air fryer basket with oil.

3. In a bowl, mix the olive oil, cabbage slaw, vinegar, lime juice, cayenne pepper and pepper.

4. In another bowl, mix the taco seasoning and flour.

5. Coat the fish cubes with the taco seasoning mixture.

6. Add these to the air fryer basket.

7. Air fry for 10 minutes, shaking halfway through.

8. Top the corn tortillas with the fish and cabbage slaw mixture and roll them up.

Ginger Sea Bass Mix Servings: 4

Ingredients:

4 boneless sea bass fillets

2 tbsps. olive oil

1 tsp. grated ginger

1 tbsp. chopped cilantro

Black pepper

1 tbsp. balsamic vinegar

Directions:

1. Heat up a pan with the oil over medium heat, add the fish and cook for 5 minutes on each side.

2. Add the rest of the ingredients, cook everything for 5 minutes more, divide everything between plates and serve.

Nutrition Info: Calories: 267, Fat:11.2 g, Carbs:1.5 g, Protein:23 g, Sugars:0.78 g, Sodium:321.2 mg

Coconut Shrimp *Servings: 4*

Cooking Time: 6 Minutes

Ingredients:

2 eggs

1 cup unsweetened dried coconut

¼ cup coconut flour

¼ teaspoon paprika

Dash cayenne pepper

½ teaspoon sea salt

Dash freshly ground black pepper

¼ cup coconut oil

1 pound (454 g) raw shrimp, peeled, deveined, and patted dry Directions:

1. Beat the eggs in a small shallow bowl until frothy. Set aside.

2. In a separate bowl, mix together the coconut, coconut flour, paprika, cayenne pepper, sea salt, and black pepper, and stir until well incorporated.

3. Dredge the shrimp in the beaten eggs, then coat the shrimp in the coconut mixture. Shake off any excess.

4. Heat the coconut oil in a large skillet over medium-high heat.

5. Add the shrimp and cook for 3 to 6 minutes, stirring occasionally, or until the flesh is totally pink and opaque.

6. Transfer the cooked shrimp to a plate lined with paper towels to drain. Serve warm.

Nutrition Info: calories: 278 ; fat: 1.9g ; protein: 19.2g ; carbs: 5.8g ; fiber: 3.1g ; sugar: 2.3g; sodium: 556mg

Pork With Nutmeg Squash Servings: 4

Cooking Time: 35 Minutes

Ingredients:

1-pound pork stew meat, cubed

1 butternut squash, peeled and cubed

1 yellow onion, chopped

2 tablespoons olive oil

2 garlic cloves, minced

½ teaspoon garam masala

½ teaspoon nutmeg, ground

1 teaspoon chili flakes, crushed

1 tablespoon balsamic vinegar

A pinch of sea salt and black pepper

Directions:

1. Heat up a pan with the oil over medium-high heat, add the onion and the garlic and sauté for 5 minutes.

2. Add the meat and brown for another 5 minutes.

3. Add the rest of the ingredients, toss, cook over medium heat for 25 minutes, divide between plates and serve.

Nutrition Info: calories 348, fat 18.2, fiber 2.1, carbs 11.4, protein 34.3

Spiced Broccoli, Cauliflower, And Tofu With Red Onion

Servings: 2

Cooking Time: 25 Minutes

Ingredients:

2 cups broccoli florets

2 cups cauliflower florets

1 medium red onion, diced

3 tablespoons extra-virgin olive oil

1 teaspoon salt

¼ teaspoon freshly ground black pepper

1-pound firm tofu, cut into 1-inch dice

1 garlic clove, minced

1 (¼-inch) piece fresh ginger, minced

Directions:

1. Preheat the oven to 400°F.

2. Combine the broccoli, cauliflower, onion, oil, salt, and pepper on a large rimmed baking sheet, and mix well.

3. Roast until the vegetables have softened, 10 to 15 minutes.

4. Add the tofu, garlic, and ginger. Roast within 10 minutes.

5. Gently mix the ingredients on the baking sheet to combine the tofu with the vegetables and serve.

Nutrition Info: Calories 210 Total Fat: 15g Total Carbohydrates: 11g Sugar: 4g Fiber: 4g Protein: 12g Sodium: 626mg

Beans And Salmon Pan _Servings: 4_

Cooking Time: 25 Minutes

Ingredients:

1 cup canned black beans, drained and rinsed 4 garlic cloves, minced

1 yellow onion, chopped

2 tablespoons olive oil

4 salmon fillets, boneless

½ teaspoon coriander, ground

1 teaspoon turmeric powder

2 tomatoes, cubed

½ cup chicken stock

A pinch of salt and black pepper

½ teaspoon cumin seeds

1 tablespoon chives, chopped

Directions:

1. Heat up a pan with the oil over medium heat, add the onion and the garlic and sauté for 5 minutes.

2. Add the fish and sear it for 2 minutes on each side.

3. Add the beans and the other ingredients, toss gently and cook for 10 minutes more.

4. Divide the mix between plates and serve right away for lunch.

Nutrition Info: calories 219, fat 8, fiber 8, carbs 12, protein 8

Carrot Soup _Servings: 4_

Cooking Time: 40 Minutes

Ingredients:

1 cup Butternut Squash, chopped

1 tbsp. Olive Oil

1 tbsp. Turmeric Powder

14 ½ oz. Coconut Milk, light

3 cups Carrot, chopped

1 Leek, rinsed & sliced

1 tbsp. Ginger, grated

3 cups Vegetable Broth

1 cup Fennel, chopped

Salt & Pepper, to taste

2 cloves of Garlic, minced

Directions:

1. Start by heating a Dutch oven over medium-high heat.

2. To this, spoon in the oil and then stir in fennel, squash, carrots, and leek. Mix well.

3. Now, sauté it for 4 to 5 minutes or until softened.

4. Next, add turmeric, ginger, pepper, and garlic to it. Cook for another 1 to 2 minutes.

5. Then, pour the broth and coconut milk to it. Combine well.

6. After that, bring the mixture to a boil and cover the Dutch oven.

7. Allow it to simmer for 20 minutes.

8. Once cooked, transfer the mixture to a high-speed blender and blend for 1 to 2 minutes or until you get a creamy smooth soup.

9. Check for seasoning and spoon in more salt and pepper if needed.

Nutrition Info: Calories: 210.4KcalProteins: 2.11gCarbohydrates: 25.64gFat: 10.91g

Healthy Pasta Salad Servings: 6

Cooking Time: 10 Minutes

Ingredients:

1 package of gluten-free fusilli pasta

1 cup of grape tomatoes, sliced

1 handful of fresh cilantro, chopped

1 cup of olives, halved

1 cup of fresh basil, chopped

½ cup of olive oil

Sea salt to taste

Directions:

1. Whisk together the olive oil, chopped basil, cilantro, and sea salt. Set aside.

2. Cook the pasta according to package directions, strain, and rinse.

3. Combine the pasta with the tomatoes and olives.

4. Add the olive oil mixture, and toss until well combined.

<u>Nutrition Info:</u> Total Carbohydrates 66g Dietary Fiber: 5g Protein: 13g Total Fat: 23g Calories: 525

Chickpea Curry Servings: 4 To 6

Cooking Time: 25 Minutes

Ingredients:

2 × 15 oz. Chickpeas, washed, drained & cooked 2 tbsp. Olive Oil

1 tbsp. Turmeric Powder

½ of 1 Onion, diced

1 tsp. Cayenne, grounded

4 Garlic cloves, minced

2 tsp. Chili Powder

15 oz. Tomato Puree

Black Pepper, as needed

2 tbsp. Tomato Paste

1 tsp. Cayenne, grounded

½ tbsp. Maple Syrup

½ of 15 oz. can of Coconut Milk

2 tsp. Cumin, grounded

2 tsp. Smoked Paprika

Directions:

1. Heat a large skillet over medium-high heat. To this, spoon in the oil.

2. Once the oil becomes hot, stir in the onion and cook for 3 to 4 minutes or until softened.

3. Next, spoon in the tomato paste, maple syrup, all seasonings, tomato puree, and garlic into it. Mix well.

4. Then, add the cooked chickpeas to it along with coconut milk, black pepper, and salt.

5. Now, give everything a good stir and allow it to simmer for 8 to 10 minutes or until thickened.

6. Drizzle lime juice over it and garnish with cilantro, if desired.

Nutrition Info: Calories: 224KcalProteins: 15.2gCarbohydrates: 32.4gFat: 7.5g

Ground Meat Stroganoff_Ingredients:

1 lb lean ground meat

1 little onion diced

1 clove garlic minced

3/4 lb new mushrooms cut

3 tablespoons flour

2 cups meat stock

salt and pepper to taste

2 teaspoons Worcestershire sauce

3/4 cup sharp cream

2 tablespoons new parsley

Directions:

1. Dark colored ground hamburger, onion and garlic (making an effort not to split it up something over the top) in a dish until no pink remains. Channel fat.

2. Include cut mushrooms and cook 2-3 minutes. Mix in flour and cook 1 progressively minute.

3. Include stock, Worcestershire sauce, salt and pepper and heat to the point of boiling. Lessen warmth and stew on low 10 minutes.

Cook egg noodles as indicated by bundle headings.

4. Expel meat blend from the warmth, mix in sharp cream and parsley.

5. Serve over egg noodles.

Saucy Short Ribs Servings: 4

Cooking Time: 65 Minutes

Ingredients:

2 lbs. beef short ribs

1 ½ tsp olive oil

1 ½ tbsp soy sauce

1 tbsp Worcestershire sauce

1 tbsp stevia

1 ¼ cups onion chopped.

1 tsp garlic minced

1/2 cup red wine

⅓ cup ketchup, sugar-free

Salt and black pepper to taste

Directions:

1. Slice the ribs into 3 segments and rub them with black pepper and salt.

2. Add oil to the Instant Pot and hit Sauté.

3. Place the ribs in the oil and sear for 5 minutes per side.

4. Toss in onion and sauté for 4 minutes.

5. Stir in garlic and cook for 1 minute.

6. Whisk rest of the ingredients in a bowl and pour over the ribs.

7. Put on its pressure lid and cook for 55 minutes on Manual mode at High pressure.

8. Once done, release the pressure naturally then remove the lid.

9. Serve warm.

Nutrition Info: Calories 555, Carbs 12.8g, Protein 66.7g, Fat 22.3g, Fiber 0.9g

Chicken And Gluten-free Noodle Soup

Servings: 4

Cooking Time: 25 Minutes

Ingredients:

¼ cup extra-virgin olive oil

3 celery stalks, cut into ¼-inch slices

2 medium carrots, cut into ¼-inch dice

1 small onion, cut into ¼-inch dice

1 fresh rosemary sprig

4 cups chicken broth

8 ounces gluten-free penne

1 teaspoon salt

¼ teaspoon freshly ground black pepper

2 cups diced rotisserie chicken

¼ cup finely chopped fresh flat-leaf parsley

Directions:

1. Heat-up the oil over high heat in a large pot.

2. Put the celery, carrots, onion, and rosemary and sauté until softened, 5 to 7 minutes.

3. Add the broth, penne, salt, and pepper and boil.

4. Simmer and cook until the penne is tender, 8 to 10 minutes.

5. Remove and discard the rosemary sprig, and add the chicken and parsley.

6. Reduce the heat to low. Cook within 5 minutes, and serve.

Nutrition Info: Calories 485 Total Fat: 18g Total Carbohydrates: 47g Sugar: 4g Fiber: 7g Protein: 33g Sodium: 1423mg

Lentil Curry _Servings: 4_

Cooking Time: 40 Minutes

Ingredients:

2 tsp. Mustard Seeds

1 tsp. Turmeric, grounded

1 cup Lentils, soaked

2 tsp. Cumin Seeds

1 Tomato, large & chopped

1 Yellow Onion, sliced finely

4 cups Water

Sea Salt, as needed

2 Carrots, sliced into half-moons

3 handful of Spinach leaves, shredded

1 tsp. Ginger, minced

½ tsp. Chili Powder

2 tbsp. Coconut Oil

Directions:

1. First, place the mung beans and water in a deep saucepan over medium-high heat.

2. Now, bring the beans mixture to a boil and allow it to simmer.

3. Simmer within 20 to 30 minutes or until the mung beans are softened.

4. Then, heat the coconut oil in a large saucepan over medium heat and stir in the mustard seeds and cumin seeds.

5. If the mustard seeds pop, put the onions. Sauté the onions for 4

minutes or until they softened.

6. Spoon in the garlic and continue sautéing for another 1 minute.

Once aromatic, spoon in the turmeric and chili powder to it.

7. Then, add the carrot and tomato—Cook for 6 minutes or until softened.

8. Finally, add the cooked lentils to it and give everything a good stir.

9. Stir in the spinach leaves and sauté until wilted. Remove from heat. Serve it warm and enjoy.

Nutrition Info: Calories 290Kcal Proteins: 14g Carbohydrates: 43g Fat: 8g

Chicken And Snap Pea Stir-fry Servings: 4

Cooking Time: 10 Minutes

Ingredients:

1 ¼ cups boneless skinless chicken breast, thinly sliced 3 tablespoons fresh cilantro, chopped

2 tablespoons vegetable oil

2 tablespoons of sesame seeds

1 bunch scallions, thinly sliced

2 teaspoons Sriracha

2 garlic cloves, minced

2 tablespoons rice vinegar

1 bell pepper, thinly sliced

3 tablespoons soy sauce

2½ cups snap peas

Salt, to taste

Freshly ground black pepper, to taste

Directions:

1. Heat-up the oil in a pan over medium heat. Add garlic and thinly sliced scallions. Cook for a minute and then add 2 ½ cups snap peas along with bell pepper. Cook until tender, just for about 3-4 minutes.

2. Add chicken and cook for about 4-5 minutes, or until thoroughly cooked.

3. Add in 2 teaspoons Sriracha, 2 tablespoons of sesame seeds, 3

tablespoons soy sauce, and 2 tablespoons rice vinegar. Toss everything until well-combined. Simmer within 2-3 minutes over low heat.

4. Add 3 tablespoons of chopped cilantro and stir well. Transfer, and sprinkle with extra sesame seeds and cilantro, if needed. Enjoy!

<u>Nutrition Info:</u> 228 calories 11 g fat 11 g total carbs 20 g protein

Juicy Broccolini With Anchovy Almonds

Servings: 6

Cooking Time: 10 Minutes

Ingredients:

2 bunches of broccolini, trimmed

1 tablespoon extra-virgin olive oil

1 long fresh red chili, deseeded, finely chopped 2 garlic cloves, thinly sliced

¼ cup natural almonds, coarsely chopped

2 teaspoons lemon rind, finely grated

A squeeze of lemon juice, fresh

4 anchovies in oil, chopped

Directions:

1. Warm the oil until hot in a large saucepan. Add the drained anchovies, garlic, chili, and lemon rind. Cook until aromatic, for 30

seconds, stirring frequently. Add the almond & continue to cook for a minute more, stirring frequently. Remove from the heat & add a squeeze of fresh lemon juice.

2. Then place the broccolini in a steamer basket set over a saucepan of simmering water. Cover & cook until crisp-tender, for 2

to 3 minutes. Drain well and then transfer to a large-sized serving plate. Top with the almond mixture. Enjoy.

Nutrition Info: kcal 350 Fat: 7 g Fiber: 3 g Protein: 6 g

Shiitake And Spinach Pattie *Servings: 8*

Cooking Time: 15 Minutes

Ingredients:

1 ½ cups shiitake mushrooms, minced

1 ½ cups spinach, chopped

3 garlic cloves, minced

2 onions, minced

4 tsp. olive oil

1 egg

1 ½ cups quinoa, cooked

1 ½ tsp. Italian seasoning

1/3 cup toasted sunflower seeds, ground

1/3 cup Pecorino cheese, grated

Directions:

1. Heat olive oil in a saucepan. Once hot, sauté shiitake mushrooms for 3 minutes or until lightly seared. Add in garlic and onion. Sauté for 2 minutes or until fragrant and translucent. Set aside.

2. In the same saucepan, heat the remaining olive oil. Add in spinach. Reduce heat, then simmer for 1 minute, drain and transfer to a strainer.

3. Chop spinach finely and add into the mushroom mixture. Add egg into the spinach mixture. Fold in cooked quinoa—season with Italian seasoning, then mix until well combined. Sprinkle sunflower seeds and cheese.

4. Divide the spinach mixture into patties—Cook patties within 5

minutes or until firm and golden brown. Serve with burger bread.

Nutrition Info: Calories 43 Carbs: 9g Fat: 0g Protein: 3g

Broccoli Cauliflower Salad Servings: 6

Cooking Time: 20 Minutes

Ingredients:

¼ tsp. Black Pepper, grounded

3 cups Cauliflower Florets

1 tbsp. Vinegar

1 tsp. Honey

8 cups Kale, chopped

3 cups Broccoli Florets

4 tbsp. Extra Virgin Olive Oil

½ tsp. Salt

1 ½ tsp. Dijon Mustard

1 tsp. Honey

½ cup Cherries, dried

1/3 cup Pecans, chopped

1 cup Manchego cheese, shaved

Directions:

1. Preheat the oven to 450 °F and place a baking sheet in the middle rack.

2. After that, place cauliflower and broccoli florets in a large bowl.

3. To this, spoon in half of the salt, two tablespoons of the oil and pepper. Toss well.

4. Now, transfer the mixture to the preheated sheet and bake it for 12 minutes while flipping it once in between.

5. Once it becomes tender and golden in color, remove it from the oven and allow it to cool completely.

6. In the meantime, mix the remaining two tablespoons of oil, vinegar, honey, mustard, and salt in another bowl.

7. Brush this mixture over the kale leaves by messaging the leaves with your hands. Set it aside for 3 to 5 minutes.

8. Finally, stir in the roasted vegetables, cheese, cherries, and pecan to the broccoli-cauliflower salad.

<u>Nutrition Info:</u> Calories: 259KcalProteins: 8.4gCarbohydrates: 23.2gFat: 16.3g

Chicken Salad With Chinese Touch *Servings: 3*

Cooking Time: 25 Minutes

Ingredients:

1 Medium green onion (thinly sliced)

2 Boneless chicken breasts

2tbsp Soya sauce

¼ Teaspoon white pepper

1tbsp sesame oil

4 cups romaine lettuce (chopped)

1 cup cabbage (shredded)

¼ Cup small cubes carrots

¼ Cup thin sliced almonds

¼ Cup noodles (only for serving)

For Preparing Chinese Dressing:

1 Minced garlic clove

1 Teaspoon soy sauce

1tbsp sesame oil

2tbsp Rice vinegar

1tbsp Sugar

Directions:

1. Prepare Chinese dressing by whisking all ingredients in a bowl.

2. In a bowl, marinate chicken breasts with garlic, olive oil, soy sauce, and white pepper for 20 minutes.

3. Place baking dish in the preheated oven (at 225C).

4. Place chicken breasts in the baking dish and bake it almost for 20 minutes.

5. For assembling the salad, combine romaine lettuce, cabbage, carrots, and green onion.

6. For serving, place a chicken piece in a plate and salad on top of it. Pour some dressing over it alongside noodles.

Nutrition Info: Calories 130 Carbs: 10g Fat: 6g Protein: 10g

Amaranth And Quinoa Stuffed Peppers

Servings: 4

Cooking Time: 1 Hour & 10 Minutes

Ingredients:

2 tablespoons Amaranth

1 medium zucchini, trimmed, grated

2 vine-ripened tomatoes, diced

2/3 cup (approximately 135 g) quinoa

1 onion, medium-sized, chopped finely

2 crushed garlic cloves

1 teaspoon ground cumin

2 tablespoons lightly toasted sunflower seeds 75g ricotta cheese, fresh

2 tablespoons currants

4 capsicums, large, halved lengthwise & seeded 2 tablespoons flat-leaf parsley, roughly chopped Directions:

1. Line a baking tray, preferably large-sized with some baking paper (nonstick) and then preheat your oven to 350 F in advance. Fill a medium-

sized saucepan with an approximately a half-liter of water and then add the amaranth and quinoa; bring it to a boil over moderate heat. Once done, decrease the heat to low; cover & let simmer until grains turn al dente and water is absorbed, for 12 to 15

minutes. Remove from the heat & set aside.

2. In the meantime, lightly coat a large-sized frying pan with oil and heat it over medium heat. Once hot, add the onion with zucchini & cook until softened, for a couple of minutes, stirring frequently. Add the cumin and garlic; cook for a minute. Remove from the heat & set aside to cool.

3. Place the grains, onion mixture, sunflower seeds, currants, parsley, ricotta, and tomato in a mixing bowl, preferably large-sized; give the ingredients a good stir until combined well—season with pepper and salt to taste.

4. Fill the capsicums with prepared quinoa mixture & arrange them on the tray, covering the tray with aluminum foil—Bake for 17 to 20

minutes. Remove the foil & bake until the stuffing turns into golden & vegetables turn fork-tender, for 15 to 20 more minutes.

Nutrition Info: kcal 200 Fat: 8.5 g Fiber: 8 g Protein: 15 g

Crispy Cheese-crusted Fish Fillet Servings: 4

Cooking Time: 10 Minutes

Ingredients:

¼-cup whole-wheat breadcrumbs

¼-cup Parmesan cheese, grated

¼-tsp sea salt ¼-tsp ground pepper

1-Tbsp. olive oil 4-pcs tilapia fillets

Directions:

1. Preheat the oven to 375°F.

2. Stir in the breadcrumbs, Parmesan cheese, salt, pepper, and olive oil in a mixing bowl.

3. Mix well until blended thoroughly.

4. Coat the fillets with the mixture, and lay each on a lightly sprayed baking sheet.

5. Place the sheet in the oven.

6. Bake for 10 minutes until the fillets cook through and turn brownish.

<u>Nutrition Info:</u> Calories: 255Fat: 7gProtein: 15.9gCarbs: 34gFiber: 2.6g

Protein Power Beans And Green Stuffed Shells

Ingredients:

Genuine or ocean salt

Olive oil

12 oz. bundle kind sized shells (around 40) 1 lb. solidified cleaved spinach

2 to 3 cloves garlic, stripped and divided

15 to 16 oz. ricotta cheddar (ideally full fat/entire milk) 2 eggs

1 can white beans, (for example, cannellini), depleted and flushed

½ C green pesto, custom made or locally acquired Ground dark pepper

3 C (or more) marinara sauce

Ground parmesan or pecorino cheddar (discretionary) <u>Directions:</u>

1. Heat at any rate 5 quarts of water to the point of boiling in an enormous pot (or work in two littler clumps). Include a tablespoon of salt, a sprinkle of olive oil, and the shells. Bubble around 9 minutes (or until extremely still somewhat firm), blending sporadically to keep the shells isolated. Tenderly channel the shells in a colander, or scoop from the water with an opened spoon. Wash quickly with cool water. Line a rimmed heating sheet with cling wrap. At the point when the shells are sufficiently cool to deal with,

separate them by hand, dumping out extra water and putting opening up in a solitary layer on the sheet container. Spread with progressively plastic wrap once practically cool.

2. Bring a couple of quarts of water (or utilize remaining pasta water, on the off chance that you didn't dump it out) to a bubble in a similar pot. Include solidified spinach and cook three minutes on high, until delicate. Line the colander with soggy paper towels on the off chance that the openings are enormous, at that point channel the spinach. Set colander over a bowl to deplete more while you start the filling.

3. Add only the garlic to a nourishment processor and run until it's finely hacked and adhering to the sides. Scratch down the sides of the bowl, at that point include the ricotta, eggs, beans, pesto, 1½ teaspoons salt, and a few toils of pepper (a major squeeze). Press the spinach in your grasp to deplete well of outstanding water, at that point add to different fixings in the nourishment processor. Run until practically smooth, with a couple of little bits of spinach still noticeable. I lean toward not to taste subsequent to including the crude egg, yet on the off chance that you think that its fundamental taste a little and modify flavoring to taste.

4. Preheat the broiler to 350 (F) and shower or gently oil a 9 x 13" skillet, in addition to another littler goulash dish (around 8 to 10 of the shells won't fit in the 9 x 13). To fill the shells, get each shell in turn, holding it open with thumb and pointer finger of your non-predominant hand.

Scoop 3 to 4 tablespoons loading up with your other hand and scratch into the shell. The greater part of them won't look great, which is alright! Spot filled shells near one another in the readied container. Spoon sauce over the shells, leaving bits of the green filling unmistakable. Spread container with thwart and prepare for 30 minutes. Increment warmth to 375 (F), sprinkle shells with some ground parmesan (if utilizing), and heat revealed for another 5

to 10 minutes until cheddar is dissolved and abundance dampness is diminished.

5. Cool 5 to 10 minutes, at that point serve alone or with a fresh plate of mixed greens as an afterthought!

Asian Noodle Salad Ingredients:

8 ounces in length slight entire wheat pasta noodles —, for example, spaghetti (use soba noodles to make gluten free) 24 ounces Mann's Broccoli Cole Slaw — 2 12-ounce sacks 4 ounces ground carrots

1/4 cup extra-virgin olive oil

1/4 cup rice vinegar

3 tablespoons nectar — utilize light agave nectar to make veggie lover

3 tablespoons smooth nutty spread

2 tablespoons low-sodium soy sauce — gluten free if necessary 1 tablespoon Sriracha pepper sauce — or garlic chile sauce, in addition to extra to taste

1 tablespoon minced new ginger

2 teaspoons minced garlic — around 4 cloves 3/4 cup broiled unsalted peanuts, — generally slashed 3/4 cup new cilantro — finely slashed

Directions:

1. Heat a huge pot of salted water to the point of boiling. Cook the noodles until still somewhat firm, as per bundle headings. Channel and flush quickly with cool water to evacuate the overabundance starch and stop the

cooking, at that point move to a huge serving bowl. Include the broccoli cole slaw and carrots.

2. While the pasta cooks, whisk together the olive oil, rice vinegar, nectar, nutty spread, soy sauce, Sriarcha, ginger, and garlic. Pour over the noodle blend and hurl to consolidate. Include the peanuts and cilantro and hurl again. Serve chilled or at room temperature with extra Sriracha sauce as wanted.

3. Formula Notes

4. Asian Noodle Salad can be served cold or at room temperature.

Store remains in the cooler in a water/air proof holder for as long as 3 days.

Salmon And Green Beans _Servings: 4_

Cooking Time: 26 Minutes

Ingredients:

2 tablespoons olive oil

1 yellow onion, chopped

4 salmon fillets, boneless

1 cup green beans, trimmed and halved

2 garlic cloves, minced

½ cup chicken stock

1 teaspoon chili powder

1 teaspoon sweet paprika

A pinch of salt and black pepper

1 tablespoon cilantro, chopped

Directions:

1. Heat up a pan with the oil over medium heat, add onion, stir and sauté for 2 minutes.

2. Add the fish and sear it for 2 minutes on each side.

3. Add the rest of the ingredients, toss gently and bake everything at 360 degrees F for 20 minutes.

4. Divide everything between plates and serve for lunch.

Nutrition Info: calories 322, fat 18.3, fiber 2, carbs 5.8, protein 35.7

Cheesy Stuffed Chicken Ingredients:

2 scallions (meagerly cut)

2 seeded jalapeños (meagerly cut)

1/4 c. cilantro

1 tsp. lime pizzazz

4 oz. Monterey Jack cheddar (coarsely ground) 4 little boneless, skinless chicken bosoms

3 tbsp. olive oil

Salt

Pepper

3 tbsp. lime juice

2 ringer peppers (daintily cut)

1/2 little red onion (meagerly cut)

5 c. torn romaine lettuce

Directions:

1. Warmth broiler to 450°F. In bowl, consolidate scallions and seeded jalapeños, 1/4 cup cilantro (cleaved) and lime get-up-and-go, at that point hurl with Monterey Jack cheddar.

2. Supplement blade into thickest piece of every one of boneless, skinless chicken bosoms and move to and fro to make 2 1/2-inch pocket that is as wide as conceivable without experiencing. Stuff chicken with cheddar blend.

3. Warmth 2 tablespoons olive oil in enormous skillet on medium.

Season chicken with salt and pepper and cook until brilliant darker on 1 side, 3 to 4 minutes. Turn chicken over and broil until cooked through, 10 to 12 minutes.

4. In the interim, in huge bowl, whisk together lime juice, 1

tablespoon olive oil and 1/2 teaspoon salt. Include ringer peppers and red onion and let sit 10 minutes, hurling sporadically. Hurl with romaine lettuce and 1 cup new cilantro. Present with chicken and lime wedges.

Arugula With Gorgonzola Dressing Servings: 4

Cooking Time: 0 Minutes

Ingredients:

1 bunch of arugulas, cleaned

1 pear, sliced thinly

1 tablespoon fresh lemon juice

1 garlic clove, bruised

1/3 cup Gorgonzola cheese, crumbled

1/4 cup vegetable stock, reduced-sodium

Freshly ground pepper

4 teaspoons olive oil

1 tablespoon of cider vinegar

Directions:

1. Put the pear slices and lemon juice in a bowl. Toss to coat.

Arrange the pear slices, along with the arugula, on a platter.

2. In a bowl, combine the vinegar, oil, cheese, broth, pepper, and garlic. Leave for 5 minutes, remove the garlic. Put the dressing, then serve.

Nutrition Info: Calories 145 Carbs: 23g Fat: 4g Protein: 6g

Cabbage Soup _Servings: 6_

Cooking Time: 35 Minutes

Ingredients:

1 yellow onion, chopped

1 green cabbage head, shredded

2 tablespoons olive oil

5 cups veggie stock

1 carrot, peeled and grated

A pinch of salt and black pepper

1 tablespoon cilantro, chopped

2 teaspoons thyme, chopped

½ teaspoon smoked paprika

½ teaspoon hot paprika

1 tablespoon lemon juice

Cauliflower Rice Servings: 4

Cooking Time: 10 Minutes

Ingredients:

¼ cup Cooking Oil

1 tbsp. Coconut Oil

1 tbsp. Coconut Sugar

4 cups Cauliflower, broken down into florets ½ tsp. Salt

Directions:

1. First, process the cauliflower in a food processor and process it for 1 to 2 minutes.

2. Heat-up the oil in a large skillet over medium heat, then spoon in the riced cauliflower, coconut sugar, and salt to the pan.

3. Combine them well and cook them for 4 to 5 minutes or until the cauliflower is slightly soft.

4. Finally, pour the coconut milk and enjoy it.

Nutrition Info: Calories 108Kcal Proteins:27.1g Carbohydrates: 11g Fat: 6g

Feta Frittata & Spinach Servings: 4

Cooking Time: 10 Minutes

Ingredients:

½ small brown onion

250g baby spinach

½ cup feta cheese

1 tbsp garlic paste

4 beaten eggs

Seasoning Mix

Salt & Pepper according to taste

1 tbsp olive oil

Directions:

1. Add finely chop an onion in oil and cook it on medium flame.

2. Add spinach in light brown onions and toss it for 2 min.

3. In eggs, add the mixture of cold spinach and onions.

4. Now add garlic paste, salt, and pepper and mix the mixture.

5. Cook this mixture on low flame and stir eggs gently.

6. Add feta cheese on the eggs and place the pan under the already preheat grill.

7. Cook it almost for 2 to 3 minutes until the frittata is brown.

8. Serve this feta frittata hot or cold.

Nutrition Info: Calories 210 Carbs: 5g Fat: 14g Protein: 21g

Fiery Chicken Pot Stickers Ingredients:

1-pound ground chicken

1/2 cup destroyed cabbage

1 carrot, stripped and destroyed

2 cloves garlic, squeezed

2 green onions, meagerly cut

1 tablespoon diminished sodium soy sauce

1 tablespoon hoisin sauce

1 tablespoon naturally ground ginger

2 teaspoons sesame oil

1/4 teaspoon ground white pepper

36 won ton wrappers

2 tablespoons vegetable oil

FOR THE HOT CHILI OIL SAUCE:

1/2 cup vegetable oil

1/4 cup dried red chillies, squashed

2 cloves garlic, minced

Directions:

1. Warmth vegetable oil in a little pan over medium warmth. Mix in squashed peppers and garlic, mixing every so often, until the oil arrives at 180 degrees F, around 8-10 minutes; put in a safe spot.

2. In an enormous bowl, join chicken, cabbage, carrot, garlic, green onions, soy sauce, hoisin sauce, ginger, sesame oil and white pepper.

3. To collect the dumplings, place wrappers on a work surface.

Spoon 1 tablespoon of the chicken blend into the focal point of every wrapper. Utilizing your finger, rub the edges of the wrappers with water. Crease the mixture over the filling to make a half-moon shape, squeezing the edges to seal.

4. Warmth vegetable oil in a huge skillet over medium warmth.

Include pot stickers in a solitary layer and cook until brilliant and fresh, around 2-3 minutes for each side.

5. Serve promptly with hot stew oil sauce.

Garlic Shrimps With Gritted Cauliflower

Servings: 2

Cooking Time: 15 Minutes

Ingredients:

For Preparing Shrimps

1 Pound Shrimps

2-3tbsp Cajun seasoning

Salt

1tbsp Butter/Ghee

For Preparing Cauliflower Grits

2tbsp Ghee

12-Ounces of Cauliflower

1 Garlic clove

Salt-to-taste

Directions:

1. Boil cauliflower and garlic in 8ounces of water on medium flame until it's tender.

2. Blend tender cauliflower in the food processor with ghee. Add steaming water gradually for the right consistency.

3. Sprinkle 2tbsp of Cajun seasoning on shrimps and marinate.

4. In a large skillet, take 3tbsp of ghee and cook shrimps on medium flame.

5. Place a large spoon of cauliflower grits in bowl top up with fried shrimps.

Nutrition Info: Calories 107 Carbs: 1g Fat: 3g Protein: 20g

Broccoli Tuna Servings: 1

Cooking Time: 10 Minutes

Ingredients:

1 tsp. Extra Virgin Olive Oil

3oz. Tuna in water, preferably light & chunky, drained 1 tbsp. Walnuts, chopped coarsely

2 cups Broccoli, chopped finely

½ tsp. Hot Sauce

Directions:

1. Begin by mixing broccoli, seasoning & tuna in a large-sized mixing bowl until they are well combined.

2. Then, microwave the veggies in the oven for 3 minutes or until tender

3. Then, stir in the walnuts and olive oil to the bowl and mix well.

4. Serve and enjoy.

Nutrition Info: Calories 259Kcal Proteins:27.1g Carbohydrates: 12.9g Fat: 12.4g

Butternut Squash Soup With Shrimp Servings: 4

Cooking Time: 20 Minutes

Ingredients:

3 tablespoons unsalted butter

1 small red onion, finely chopped

1 garlic clove, sliced

1 teaspoon turmeric

1 teaspoon salt

¼ teaspoon freshly ground black pepper

3 cups vegetable broth

2 cups peeled butternut squash cut into ¼-inch dice 1-pound cooked peeled shrimp, thawed if necessary 1 cup unsweetened almond milk

¼ cup slivered almonds (optional)

2 tablespoons finely chopped fresh flat-leaf parsley 2 teaspoons grated or minced lemon zest

Directions:

1. Dissolve the butter over high heat in a large pot.

2. Add the onion, garlic, turmeric, salt, and pepper and sauté until the vegetables are soft and translucent, 5 to 7 minutes.

3. Add the broth and squash and boil.

4. Simmer within 5 minutes.

5. Add the shrimp and almond milk and cook until heated through about 2 minutes.

6. Sprinkle with the almonds (if using), parsley, and lemon zest and serve.

Nutrition Info: Calories 275 Total Fat: 12g Total Carbohydrates: 12g Sugar: 3g Fiber: 2g Protein: 30g Sodium: 1665mg

Tasty Turkey Baked Balls _Servings: 6_

Cooking Time: 30 Minutes

Ingredients:

1 pound ground turkey

½-cup fresh breadcrumbs, white or whole wheat ½-cup Parmesan cheese, freshly grated

½-Tbsp. basil, freshly chopped

½-Tbsp. oregano, freshly chopped

1-pc large egg, beaten

1-Tbsp. parsley, freshly chopped

3-Tbsp.s milk or water

A dash of salt and pepper

A pinch of freshly grated nutmeg

Directions:

1. Preheat your oven to 350°F.

2. Line two baking pans with parchment paper.

3. Stir in all of the ingredients in a large mixing bowl.

4. Form 1-inch balls from the mixture and place each ball in the baking pan.

5. Put the pan in the oven.

6. Bake for 30 minutes, or until the turkey cooks through and the surfaces turn brown.

7. Turn the meatballs once halfway into the cooking.

Nutrition Info: Calories: 517 CalFat: 17.2 g Protein: 38.7 g Carbs: 52.7 gFiber: 1 g

Clear Clam Chowder *Servings: 4*

Cooking Time: 15 Minutes

Ingredients:

2 tablespoons unsalted butter

2 medium carrots, cut into ½-inch pieces

2 celery stalks, thinly sliced

1 small red onion, cut into ¼-inch dice

2 garlic cloves, sliced

2 cups vegetable broth

1 (8-ounce) bottle clam juice

1 (10-ounce) can clams

½ teaspoon dried thyme

½ teaspoon salt

¼ teaspoon freshly ground black pepper

Directions:

1. Dissolve the butter in a large pot, over high heat.

2. Add the carrots, celery, onion, and garlic and sauté until slightly softened 2 to 3 minutes.

3. Add the broth and clam juice and boil.

4. Simmer and cook until the carrots are soft, 3 to 5 minutes.

5. Stir in the clams and their juices, thyme, salt, and pepper, heat through for 2 to 3 minutes, and serve.

Nutrition Info: Calories 156 Total Fat: 7g Total Carbohydrates: 7g Sugar: 3g Fiber: 1g Protein: 14g Sodium: 981mg

Rice And Chicken Pot Servings: 4

Cooking Time: 25 Minutes

Ingredients:

1 lb. free-range chicken breast, boneless, skinless ¼ cup of brown rice

¾ lb. mushrooms of choice, sliced

1 leek, chopped

¼ cup almonds, chopped

1 cup of water

1 Tbsp. olive oil

1 cup green beans

½ cup apple cider vinegar

2 Tbsp. all-purpose flour

1 cup milk, low fat

¼ cup Parmesan cheese, freshly grated

¼ cup sour cream

Pinch of sea salt, add more if needed

ground black pepper, to taste

Directions:

1. Pour brown rice into a pot. Add in water. Cover and bring to a boil. Lower the heat, then simmer for 30 minutes or until rice is cooked.

2. Meanwhile, in a skillet, add the chicken breast and pour just enough water to cover—season with salt. Boil the mixture, then reduce heat and allow to simmer for 10 minutes.

3. Shred the chicken. Set aside.

4. Warm the olive oil. Cook leeks until tender. Add in mushrooms.

5. Pour apple cider vinegar into the mixture. Sauté the mixture until the vinegar has evaporated. Add in flour and milk into the skillet.

Sprinkle Parmesan cheese and add in sour cream. Season with black pepper.

6. Preheat the oven to 350 degrees F. lightly grease a casserole dish with oil.

7. Spread cooked rice in the casserole dish, then the shredded chicken and green beans on top. Add mushrooms and leeks sauce.

Put almonds on top.

8. Bake within 20 minutes or until golden brown. Allow cooling before serving.

Nutrition Info: Calories 401 Carbs: 54g Fat: 12g Protein: 20g

Sautéed Shrimp Jambalaya Jumble Servings: 4

Cooking Time: 30 Minutes

Ingredients:

10-oz. medium shrimp, peeled

¼-cup celery, chopped ½-cup onion, chopped

1-Tbsp. oil or butter ¼-tsp garlic, minced

¼-tsp onion salt or sea salt

⅓-cup tomato sauce ½-tsp smoked paprika

½-tsp Worcestershire sauce

⅔-cup carrots, chopped

1¼-cups chicken sausage, precooked and diced 2-cups lentils, soaked overnight and precooked 2-cups okra, chopped

A dash of crushed red pepper and black pepper Parmesan cheese, grated for topping (optional) Directions:

1. Sauté the shrimp, celery, and onion with oil in a pan placed over medium-high heat for five minutes, or until the shrimp turn pinkish.

2. Add in the rest of the ingredients, and sauté further for 10

minutes, or until the veggies are tender.

3. To serve, divide the jambalaya mixture equally among four serving bowls.

4. Top with pepper and cheese, if desired.

Nutrition Info: Calories: 529Fat: 17.6gProtein: 26.4gCarbs: 98.4gFiber: 32.3g

Chicken Chili <u>Servings: 6</u>

Cooking Time: 1 Hour

Ingredients:

1 yellow onion, chopped

2 tablespoons olive oil

2 garlic cloves, minced

1-pound chicken breast, skinless, boneless and cubed 1 green bell pepper, chopped

2 cups chicken stock

1 tablespoon cocoa powder

2 tablespoons chili powder

1 teaspoon smoked paprika

1 cup canned tomatoes, chopped

1 tablespoon cilantro, chopped

A pinch of salt and black pepper

Directions:

1. Heat up a pot with the oil over medium heat, add the onion and the garlic and sauté for 5 minutes.

2. Add the meat and brown it for 5 minutes more.

3. Add the rest of the ingredients, toss, cook over medium heat for 40 minutes.

4. Divide the chili into bowls and serve for lunch.

<u>Nutrition Info:</u> calories 300, fat 2, fiber 10, carbs 15, protein 11

Garlic And Lentil Soup Servings: 4

Cooking Time: 15 Minutes

Ingredients:

2 tablespoons extra-virgin olive oil

2 medium carrots, thinly sliced

1 small white onion, cut into ¼-inch dice

2 garlic cloves, thinly sliced

1 teaspoon ground cinnamon

1 teaspoon salt

¼ teaspoon freshly ground black pepper

3 cups vegetable broth

1 (15-ounce) can lentils, drained and rinsed 1 tablespoon minced or grated orange zest

¼ cup chopped walnuts (optional)

2 tablespoons finely chopped fresh flat-leaf parsley Directions:

1. Heat-up the oil over high heat in a large pot.

2. Put the carrots, onion, and garlic and sauté until softened, 5 to 7 minutes.

3. Put the cinnamon, salt, and pepper and stir to coat the vegetables, 1 to 2 minutes evenly.

4. Put the broth and boil. Simmer, then put the lentils, and cook until within 1 minute.

5. Stir in the orange zest and serve, sprinkled with the walnuts (if using) and parsley.

Nutrition Info: Calories 201 Total Fat: 8g Total Carbohydrates: 22g Sugar: 4g Fiber: 8g Protein: 11g Sodium: 1178mg

Zesty Zucchini & Chicken In Classic Santa Fe Stir-fry

Servings: 2

Cooking Time: 15 Minutes

Ingredients:

1-Tbsp. olive oil

2-pcs chicken breasts, sliced

1-pc onion, small, diced

2-cloves garlic, minced 1-pc zucchini, diced ½- cup carrots, shredded

1-tsp paprika, smoked 1-tsp cumin, ground

½-tsp chili powder ¼-tsp sea salt

2-Tbsp. fresh lime juice

¼-cup cilantro, freshly chopped

Brown rice or quinoa, when serving

Directions:

1. Sauté the chicken with olive oil for about 3 minutes until the chicken turns brown. Set aside.

2. Use the same wok and add the onion and garlic.

3. Cook until the onion is tender.

4. Add in the carrots and zucchini.

5. Stir the mixture, and cook further for about a minute.

6. Add all the seasonings into the mix, and stir to cook for another minute.

7. Return the chicken in the wok, and pour in the lime juice.

8. Stir to cook until everything cooks through.

9. To serve, place the mixture over cooked rice or quinoa and top with the freshly chopped cilantro.

<u>Nutrition Info:</u> Calories: 191Fat: 5.3gProtein: 11.9gCarbs: 26.3gFiber: 2.5g

Tilapia Tacos With Awesome Ginger-sesame Slaw

Servings: 4

Cooking Time: 5 Hours

Ingredients:

1 tsp fresh ginger, grated

Salt and freshly cracked black pepper to taste 1 tsp stevia

1 tbsp soy sauce

1 tbsp olive oil

1 tbsp lemon juice

1 tbsp plain yogurt

1½lb tilapia fillets

1 cup coleslaw mix

Directions:

1. Switch on the instant pot, add all the ingredients in it, except for tilapia fillets and coleslaw mix, and stir until well combined.

2. Then add fillets, toss until well coated, shut with the lid, press the 'slow cook' button, and cook for 5 hours, flipping the fillets halfway through.

3. When done, transfer fillets to a dish and let cool completely.

4. For meal prep, distribute coleslaw mix between four air-tight containers, add tilapia and refrigerate for up to three days.

5. When ready to eat, reheat tilapia in the microwave until hot and then serve with coleslaw.

Nutrition Info: Calories 278, Total Fat 7.4g, Total Carbs 18.6g, Protein 35.9g, Sugar 1.2g, Fiber 8.2g, Sodium 194mg

Curry Lentil Stew *Servings: 4*

Cooking Time: 15 Minutes

Ingredients:

1 tablespoon of olive oil

1 onion, chopped

2 garlic cloves, minced

1 tablespoon of organic curry seasoning

4 cups of organic low-sodium vegetable broth 1 cup of red lentils

2 cups of butternut squash, cooked

1 cup of kale

1 teaspoon of turmeric

Sea salt to taste

Directions:

1. Sauté the olive oil with the onion and garlic in a large pot over medium heat, add. Sauté for 3 minutes.

2. Add in the organic curry seasoning, vegetable broth, and lentils, and bring to a boil—Cook for 10 minutes.

3. Stir in the cooked butternut squash and kale.

4. Add in the turmeric and sea salt to taste.

5. Serve warm.

<u>Nutrition Info:</u> Total Carbohydrates 41g Dietary Fiber: 13g Protein: 16g Total Fat: 4g Calories: 252

Kale Caesar Salad With Grilled Chicken Wrap

Servings: 2

Cooking Time: 20 Minutes

Ingredients:

6 cups curly kale, cut into small, bite-sized pieces ½ coddled egg; cooked

8 ounces grilled chicken, thinly sliced

½ teaspoon Dijon mustard

¾ cup Parmesan cheese, finely shredded

ground black pepper

kosher salt

1 garlic clove, minced

1 cup cherry tomatoes, quartered

1/8 cup lemon juice, freshly squeezed

2 large tortillas or two Lavash flatbreads

1 teaspoon agave or honey

1/8 cup olive oil

Directions:

1. Combine half of the coddled egg with mustard, minced garlic, honey, olive oil, and lemon juice in a large-sized mixing bowl. Whisk until you get dressing like consistency. Season with pepper and salt to taste.

2. Add the cherry tomatoes, chicken and kale; gently toss until nicely coated with the dressing & then add ¼ cup of parmesan.

3. Spread out the flatbreads & evenly distribute the prepared salad on top of the wraps; sprinkle each with approximately ¼ cup of the parmesan.

4. Roll up the wraps & slice into half. Serve immediately & enjoy.

Nutrition Info: kcal 511 Fat: 29 g Fiber: 2.8 g Protein: 50 g

Spinach Bean Salad Servings: 1

Cooking Time: 5 Minutes

Ingredients:

1 cup of fresh spinach

¼ cup of canned black beans

½ cup of canned garbanzo beans

½ cup of cremini mushrooms

2 tablespoons of organic balsamic vinaigrette 1 tablespoon of olive oil

Directions:

1. Cook the cremini mushrooms with the olive oil over low, medium heat for 5 minutes, until lightly browned.

2. Assemble the salad by adding the fresh spinach to a plate and topping it with the beans, mushrooms, and the balsamic vinaigrette.

Nutrition Info: Total Carbohydrates 26gg Dietary Fiber: 8g Protein: 9g Total Fat: 15g Calories: 274

Crusted Salmon With Walnuts & Rosemary

Servings: 6

Cooking Time: 20 Minutes

Ingredients:

1 Mince garlic clove

1tbsp Dijon mustard

¼ tbsp Lemon zest

1tbsp Lemon juice

1tbsp fresh rosemary

1/2 tbsp Honey

Olive oil

Fresh parsley

3tbsp Chopped walnuts

1 Pound skinless salmon

1tbsp Fresh crushed red pepper

Salt & pepper

Lemon wedges for garnish

3tbsp Panko breadcrumbs

1tbsp extra-virgin olive oil

Directions:

1. Spread the baking sheet in the oven and preheat it at 240C.

2. In a bowl, mix mustard paste, garlic, salt, olive oil, honey, lemon juice, crushed red pepper, rosemary, pus honey.

3. Combine panko, walnuts, and oil and spread thin fish slice on the baking sheet. Spray olive oil equally on both sides of the fish.

4. Place walnut mixture on the salmon with the mustard mixture on top it.

5. Bake the salmon almost for 12 minutes. Garnish it with fresh parsley and lemon wedges and serve it hot.

Nutrition Info: Calories 227 Carbs: 0g Fat: 12g Protein: 29g

Baked Sweet Potato With Red Tahini Sauce

Servings: 4

Cooking Time: 30 Minutes

Ingredients:

15-ounces Canned Chickpeas

4 Medium-sized sweet potatoes

½ tbsp Olive oil

1 Pinch salt

1tbsp Lime juice

1/2 tbsp of cumin, coriander, and paprika powder For Garlic Herb Sauce

¼ Cup tahini sauce

½ tbsp Lime Juice

3 cloves garlic

Salt to taste

Directions:

1. Preheat the oven at 204°C. Toss chickpeas in salt, spices & olive oil. Spread them on the foil sheet.

2. Brush sweet potato thin wedges with oil and place them on marinated beans and bake.

3. For the sauce, mix all fixings in a bowl. Add some water in it, but keep it thick.

4. Remove sweet potatoes from the oven after 25 minutes.

5. Garnish this baked sweet potato chickpea salad with hot garlic sauce.

Nutrition Info: Calories 90 Carbs: 20g Fat: 0g Protein: 2g

Italian Summer Squash Soup _Servings: 4_

Cooking Time: 15 Minutes

Ingredients:

3 tablespoons extra-virgin olive oil

1 small red onion, thinly sliced

1 garlic clove, minced

1 cup shredded zucchini

1 cup shredded yellow squash

½ cup shredded carrot

3 cups vegetable broth

1 teaspoon salt

2 tablespoons finely chopped fresh basil

1 tablespoon finely chopped fresh chives

2 tablespoons pine nuts

Directions:

1. Heat-up the oil over high heat in a large pot.

2. Put the onion and garlic and sauté until softened, 5 to 7 minutes.

3. Add the zucchini, yellow squash, and carrot and sauté until softened, 1 to 2 minutes.

4. Add the broth and salt, and boil. Simmer within 1 to 2 minutes.

5. Stir in the basil and chives and serve, sprinkled with the pine nuts.

Nutrition Info: Calories 172 Total Fat: 15g Total Carbohydrates: 6g Sugar: 3g Fiber: 2g Protein: 5g Sodium: 1170mg

Saffron And Salmon Soup Servings: 4

Cooking Time: 20 Minutes

Ingredients:

¼ cup extra-virgin olive oil

2 leeks, white parts only, thinly sliced

2 medium carrots, thinly sliced

2 garlic cloves, thinly sliced

4 cups vegetable broth

1-pound skinless salmon fillets, cut into 1-inch pieces 1 teaspoon salt

¼ teaspoon freshly ground black pepper

¼ teaspoon saffron threads

2 cups baby spinach

½ cup dry white wine

2 tablespoons chopped scallions, both white and green parts 2 tablespoons finely chopped fresh flat-leaf parsley Directions:

1. Heat the oil over high in a large pot.

2. Add the leeks, carrots, and garlic and sauté until softened, 5 to 7 minutes.

3. Put the broth and boil.

4. Simmer and add the salmon, salt, pepper, and saffron. Cook until the salmon is cooked through, about 8 minutes.

5. Add the spinach, wine, scallions, and parsley and cook until the spinach has wilted, 1 to 2 minutes, and serve.

Nutrition Info: Calories 418 Total Fat: 26g Total Carbohydrates: 13g Sugar: 4g Fiber: 2g Protein: 29g Sodium: 1455mg

Thai Flavored Hot And Sour Shrimp And Mushroom Soup

Servings: 6

Cooking Time: 38 Minutes

Ingredients:

3 tbsp unsalted butter

1lb shrimp, peeled and deveined

2 tsp minced garlic

1-inch piece ginger root, peeled

1 medium onion, diced

1 red Thai chili, chopped

1 lemongrass stalk

½ tsp fresh lime zest

Salt and freshly cracked black pepper, to taste 5 cups chicken broth

1 tbsp coconut oil

½lb cremini mushrooms, sliced into wedges

1 small green zucchini

2 tbsp fresh lime juice

2 tbsp fish sauce

¼ bunch of fresh Thai basil, chopped

¼ bunch of fresh cilantro, chopped

Directions:

1. Take a large pot, place it over medium heat, add butter and when it melts, add shrimps, garlic, ginger, onion, chilies, lemongrass, and lime zest, season with salt and black pepper and cook for 3 minutes.

2. Pour in broth, simmer for 30 minutes, and then strain it.

3. Take a large skillet pan over medium heat, add oil and when hot, add mushrooms and zucchini, season more with salt and black pepper and cook for 3 minutes.

4. Add shrimp's mixture in the skillet pan, simmer for 2 minutes, drizzle with lime juice and fish sauce and cook for 1 minute.

5. Taste to adjust seasoning, then remove the pan from heat, garnish with cilantro and basil and serve.

Nutrition Info: Calories 223, Total Fat 10.2g, Total Carbs 8.7g, Protein 23g, Sugar 3.6g, Sodium 1128mg

Orzo With Sundried Tomatoes Ingredients:

1 lb boneless skinless chicken bosoms, diced into 3/4-inch pieces

1 Tbsp + 1 tsp olive oil

Salt and crisply ground dark pepper

2 cloves garlic, minced

1/4 cups (8 oz) dry orzo pasta

2 3/4 cups low-sodium chicken stock, at that point more varying (don't utilize ordinary juices, it will be excessively salty) 1/3 cup sun dried tomato parts stuffed in oil with herbs (around 12 parts. Shake off a portion of the abundance oil), hacked fine in a nourishment processor

1/2 - 3/4 cup finely destroyed parmesan cheddar, to taste 1/3 cup cleaved crisp basil

Directions:

1. Warmth 1 Tbsp olive oil in a saute container over medium-high warmth.

2. Once gleaming include chicken, season gently with salt and pepper and cook until brilliant, around 3 minutes at that point pivot to inverse sides and cook until brilliant dark colored and cooked through, around 3 minutes. Move chicken to a plate, spread with foil to keep warm.

3. Include staying 1 tsp olive oil to saute dish at that point include garlic and saute 20 seconds, or just until daintily brilliant, at that point pour in chicken juices while scraping up cooked bits from base of skillet.

4. Heat stock to the point of boiling at that point include orzo pasta, lessen warmth to medium spread skillet with cover and permit to delicately bubble 5 minutes at that point reveal, mix and keep on bubbling revealed until orzo is delicate, around 5 minutes longer, blending at times (don't stress if there's still a little juices, it will give it some saucy-ness).

5. When pasta has cooked through hurl chicken in with orzo at that point expel from heat. Include parmesan cheddar and mix until dissolved, at that point hurl in sun dried tomatoes, basil and season

with pepper (you shouldn't require any salt however include a little in the event that you'd think it needs it).

6. Add more juices to thin whenever wanted (as the pasta rests it will absorb abundance fluid and I enjoyed it with somewhat overabundance so I included somewhat more). Serve warm.

Mushroom And Beet Soup _Servings: 4_

Cooking Time: 40 Minutes

Ingredients:

2 tablespoons olive oil

1 yellow onion, chopped

2 beets, peeled and cut into large cubes

1-pound white mushrooms, sliced

2 garlic cloves, minced

1 tablespoon tomato paste

5 cups veggie stock

1 tablespoons parsley, chopped

Directions:

1. Heat up a pot with the oil over medium heat, add the onion and the garlic and sauté for 5 minutes.

2. Add the mushrooms, stir and sauté for 5 minutes more.

3. Add the beets and the other ingredients, bring to a simmer and cook over medium heat for 30 minutes more, stirring from time to time.

4. Ladle the soup into bowls and serve.

Nutrition Info: calories 300, fat 5, fiber 9, carbs 8, protein 7

Chicken Parmesan Meatballs Ingredients:

2 pounds ground chicken

3/4 cup panko breadcrumbs gluten free panko will work fine 1/4 cup finely minced onion

2 tablespoons minced parsley

2 cloves garlic minced

get-up-and-go of 1 little lemon around 1 teaspoon 2 eggs

3/4 cup destroyed Pecorino Romano or Parmesan cheddar 1 teaspoon genuine salt

1/2 teaspoon crisply ground dark pepper

1 quart Five Minute Marinara Sauce

4-6 ounces mozzarella crisply cut

Directions:

1. Preheat the stove to 400 degrees, setting the rack in the upper third of the broiler. In a huge bowl, join everything aside from the marinara and the mozzarella. Softly combine, utilizing your hands or an enormous spoon. Scoop and shape into little meatballs and spot on a foil lined heating sheet. Spot the meatballs genuinely near one another on the plate to make them

fit. Spoon about a half tablespoon of sauce over every meatball. Heat for 15 minutes.

2. Expel meatballs from the stove and increment the broiler temperature to cook. Spoon an extra half tablespoon of sauce over every meatball and top with a little square of mozzarella. (I cut the slight cuts into pieces around 1" square.) Broil an extra 3 minutes, until the cheddar has softened and turned brilliant. Present with extra sauce. Appreciate!

Meatballs Alla Parmigiana_Ingredients:

For the meatballs

1.5lbs ground hamburger (80/20)

2 Tbl crisp parsley, cleaved

3/4 cup ground parmesan cheddar

1/2 cup almond flour

2 eggs

1 tsp fit salt

1/4 tsp ground dark pepper

1/4 tsp garlic powder

1 tsp dried onion drops

1/4 tsp dried oregano

1/2 cup warm water

For the Parmigiana

1 cup simple keto marinara sauce (or any sugar free locally acquired marinara)

4 oz mozzarella cheddar

Directions:

1. Join the entirety of the meatball fixings in a huge bowl and blend well.

2. Structure into fifteen 2" meatballs.

3. Prepare at 350 degrees (F) for 20 minutes OR fry in an enormous skillet over medium warmth until cooked through. Ace tip – have a go at searing in bacon oil in the event that you have any – it includes another degree of flavor. Fricasseeing produces the brilliant dark colored shading appeared in the photographs above.

4. For the Parmigiana:

5. Spot the cooked meatballs in a stove safe dish.

6. Spoon roughly 1 Tbl sauce over every meatball.

7. Spread with roughly 1/4 oz of mozzarella cheddar each.

8. Prepare at 350 degrees (F) for 20 minutes (40 minutes if meatballs are solidified) or until warmed through and the cheddar is brilliant.

9. Embellishment with new parsley whenever wanted.

Sheet Pan Turkey Breast With Golden Vegetables

Servings: 4

Cooking Time: 45 Minutes

Ingredients:

2 tablespoons unsalted butter, at room temperature 1 medium acorn squash, seeded and thinly sliced 2 large golden beets, peeled and thinly sliced ½ medium yellow onion, thinly sliced

½ boneless, skin-on turkey breast (1 to 2 pounds) 2 tablespoons honey

1 teaspoon salt

1 teaspoon turmeric

¼ teaspoon freshly ground black pepper

1 cup chicken broth or vegetable broth

Directions:

1. Preheat the oven to 400°F. Grease the baking sheet with the butter.

2. Arrange the squash, beets, and onion in a single layer on the baking sheet. Put the turkey skin-side up. Drizzle with the honey.

Season with the salt, turmeric, and pepper, and add the broth.

3. Roast until the turkey registers 165°F in the center with an instant-read thermometer, 35 to 45 minutes. Remove, and let rest for 5 minutes.

4. Slice, and serve.

Nutrition Info: Calories 383 Total Fat: 15g Total Carbohydrates: 25g Sugar: 13g Fiber: 3g Protein: 37g Sodium: 748mg

Coconut Green Curry With Boil Rice Servings: 8

Cooking Time: 20 Minutes

Ingredients:

2tbsp Olive oil

12ounces of Tofu

2 medium sweet potatoes (cut into cubes)

Salt-to-taste

314ounces Coconut milk

4tbsp Green curry paste

3 Cups of Broccoli Florets

Directions:

1. Remove excess water from tofu and fry it on medium flame. Add salt in it and fry it for 12 minutes.

2. Cook coconut milk, green curry paste, and sweet potato on medium heat and simmer it for 5 mins.

3. Now add broccoli and tofu in it and cook it almost 5 minutes until the broccoli color changes.

4. Serve this coconut and green curry with a handful of boil rice and many raisins on top of it.

Nutrition Info: Calories 170 Carbs: 34g Fat: 2g Protein: 3g

Sweet Potato & Chicken Soup With Lentil

Servings: 6

Cooking Time: 35 Minutes

Ingredients:

10 Celery stalks

1 Home-cooked or rotisserie chicken

2 medium sweet potatoes

5-ounces French lentils

2tbsp Fresh lime juice

½ head bite-size escarole

6 thin-sliced garlic cloves

½ Cup dill (finely chop)

1tbsp Kosher Salt

2tbsp Extra virgin oil

Directions:

1. Add salt, chicken carcass, lentil, and sweet potatoes in 8 ounces of water and boil it on high flame.

2. Cook these items almost for 10-12 minutes and skim off all the foam form on it.

3. Cook garlic and celery in oil almost for 10 minutes until it is tender

& light brown, then add shredded roast chicken in it.

4. Add this mixture in the escarole soup and continuously stir it for 5

minutes on medium heat.

5. Add lemon juice and stir in dill. Serve season hot soup with salt.

Nutrition Info: Calories 310 Carbs: 45g Fat: 11g Protein: 13g

www.ingramcontent.com/pod-product-compliance
Lightning Source LLC
Chambersburg PA
CBHW071821080526
44589CB00012B/881